U0662072

高等学校专业英语教材

学术英语视听说教程
——信息技术方向

Academic English Viewing, Listening and Speaking
Information Technology

◎ 林 易 曲婧华 陈 聪 主编

电子工业出版社
Publishing House of Electronics Industry
北京·BEIJING

内 容 简 介

本书以"学术性""真实性""相关性"为原则组织内容，以"体裁分析"法为理念设计任务，着重培养学生在学术英语场景中的听说能力。本书由 12 个单元组成，每个单元围绕一个主题展开，内容涉及信息技术领域前沿学科：计算机科学、无线通信、卫星导航、物联网、人工智能、区块链、大数据、量子计算、网络安全、元宇宙、云计算和无人机。每个单元包括基础训练、科技新闻、学术讲座、学术演讲、口语练习 5 个部分，辅以听写填空、判断正误、语步识别、新闻复述、汇报展示等 12 个产出任务，旨在为学生提升学术场景中的英语听说能力打下良好基础，以及帮助学生掌握科技发展动态。

本书既适合作为本科高年级学生和研究生的英语听说教材，也可供感兴趣的读者学习参考。

图书在版编目（CIP）数据

学术英语视听说教程. 信息技术方向 / 林易，曲婧华，陈聪主编. —北京：电子工业出版社，2024.8
ISBN 978-7-121-47741-6

Ⅰ. ①学…　Ⅱ. ①林…　②曲…　③陈…　Ⅲ. ①英语－听说教学－高等学校－教材　Ⅳ. ①H319.9

中国国家版本馆 CIP 数据核字（2024）第 080126 号

责任编辑：戴晨辰　　　特约编辑：张燕虹
印　　刷：河北鑫兆源印刷有限公司
装　　订：河北鑫兆源印刷有限公司
出版发行：电子工业出版社
　　　　　北京市海淀区万寿路 173 信箱　　邮编：100036
开　　本：787×1 092　1/16　印张：9.5　字数：316 千字
版　　次：2024 年 8 月第 1 版
印　　次：2024 年 8 月第 1 次印刷
定　　价：59.00 元

凡所购买电子工业出版社图书有缺损问题，请向购买书店调换。若书店售缺，请与本社发行部联系，联系及邮购电话：（010）88254888，88258888。

质量投诉请发邮件至 zlts@phei.com.cn，盗版侵权举报请发邮件至 dbqq@phei.com.cn。

本书咨询联系方式：dcc@phei.com.cn。

本书编者

主　编　林　易　曲婧华　陈　聪

副主编　李丙午　任永山　张娅丽　李艳霞　王　臻

编　委　（按姓氏笔画排序）

　　　　张小艳　张　杰　宋德伟　林楚甜　杨璐夷

　　　　赵元元　徐若飞　彭　强

前　言

当前，新一轮科技革命和产业变革蓄势待发，以互联网、大数据、人工智能等为代表的信息技术日新月异，各国都在加快抢占信息技术战略制高点的步伐，这也给我国的高等教育提出了巨大挑战。要紧跟信息技术最新发展浪潮并在国际学术舞台上发出中国声音，就必须培养大量能够在国际舞台上用英语表达、交际和思辨的高层次科技人才。

本书旨在通过信息技术领域发展的最新动态和前沿知识，帮助学生提高真实国际学术交流语境中的英语听说能力。

本书特色如下：

（1）所选主题均来自信息技术领域的前沿学科和热点研究，如无线通信、卫星导航、人工智能、区块链、大数据、量子计算、云计算和无人机等。

（2）在内容组织方面遵循真实性原则，筛选符合学术场景和语言规范的文本，如科技新闻、学术讲座、学术演讲等。

（3）任务设计渗透"体裁分析"法，侧重结合该理论的经典分析方法，如组织结构、修辞分析、交际目的、语步识别等设计题目。

（4）通过显性、循序渐进的训练，帮助学生培养体裁意识，培养学术英语技能，实现从输入到输出的转换。

（5）本书不仅关注读者对科技和专业知识的需求，还注重将思辨性和启发性融入任务设计中。

通过本书的学习，读者不仅能更好地提升学术英语听说能力，还能掌握学科前沿术语和相关概念，并培塑科研精神与思辨能力。

本书包含配套教学资源，读者可登录华信教育资源网（www.hxedu.com.cn）注册后免费下载。

本书为第十一批"中国外语教育基金"项目"基于'体裁分析'的学术英语听说教材开发研究"（项目编号：ZGWYJYJJ11A052）的阶段性成果。

由于作者水平有限，错漏之处在所难免，恳请广大读者提出宝贵意见。

作　者

Contents

Unit 6   Blockchain

Unit 7   Big Data

Unit 8   Quantum Computing

Unit 9   Cybersecurity

Unit 10   Metaverse

Unit 11   Cloud Computing

Unit 12　Unmanned Aerial Vehicle

Unit 1

Computer Science

Science ABC

Task 1: Dictation

Directions: Listen to a recording entitled *Computer Software in Plain English* and complete the excerpt with one word in each blank.

New Words & Phrases

1. machinery: *n.* machines as a group, especially large ones 机器

2. typewriter: *n.* a machine that produces writing similar to print. It has keys that you press to make metal letters or signs hit a piece of paper through a long, narrow piece of cloth covered with ink 打字机

3. nerd: *n.* a person who is very interested in computers 电脑迷

... The problem with computers is that most of us don't speak their 1. _____. We need a translator, something that can understand our needs and put the computer to work for us. The translator is called "software", and it makes computers useful. Look at it this way. Like a typewriter, a computer without software is just a 2. _____ machine. By adding software, the computer becomes more alive, easy to use, and built for you.

Most computers have two basic kinds, the operating system, and software programs. If you've ever used a computer, you've used an operating system. From saving files to using a mouse or fixing problems, the operating system covers the 3. _____. Operating systems come with all new computers and do a lot of the same things....

To make them 4. _____ and more useful, we can add software programs. For example, if you need to edit a photo, you can add a software program that is built for that purpose. If you need to design a house, you can add a software program that lets you see the house from all sides. By adding and 5. _____ software programs, you can make the computer 6. _____ with exactly what you want to do....

Once a program is on your computer, opening it is as easy as clicking an 7. _____. But what is a software program? What's really happening when you open one? Think about it this way. Computers are really good at following 8. _____, and a software program is essentially a set of instructions that tells the computer exactly what to do. When you open a program, the computer goes to work, 9. _____ the instructions until the program is ready for you to use. The ability to add and remove software programs means that everyone's computer can be different and unique to them.

So, to review, we've talked about operating systems that take care of the basics, and software programs that make computers personalized. It's this combination that makes computers so useful… Every day, we 10. _____ on software to bring machines to life and make them personalized and useful. The next time you use a computer or cell phone, think about software's role in translating your needs into instructions that put the machine to work for you.

Task 2: True or False

Directions: Listen to a recording entitled *How Computer Memory Works* and decide if the following statements are true or false. Write down T for True and F for False.

New Words & Phrases

1. exponentially: *adv.* in a manner of rapid growth 急剧增长，呈指数增长

2. retrieve: *v.* to find and get back data or information that has been stored in the memory of a computer 检索数据

3. transistor: *n.* a small electronic device used in computers, radios, televisions, etc. for controlling an electric current as it passes along a circuit 晶体管

4. capacitor: *n.* a device used to store an electrical charge 电容器

5. nanosecond: *n.* one thousand millionth of a second 纳秒

6. cache: *n.* a part of a computer's memory that stores copies of data that is often needed while a program is running. This data can be accessed very quickly 高速缓冲存储器

7. degrade: *v.* to make something become worse, especially in quality 降低，削弱（尤指质量）

---

1. The central processing unit, or CPU, acts as the computer's brain. _____

2. The most common type of random access memory, or RAM, is SRAM. _____

3. SRAM is the fastest memory in a computer system, but also the most expensive, and takes up four times more space than DRAM. _____

4. Long-term storage device comes in three major types: magnetic storage, optical-based storage, and solid-state drives. _____

5. Computer memory degrades fairly slowly. _____

Task 3: Multiple Choices

Directions: Watch a video entitled *Inside Your Computer* and choose the best answer.

New Words & Phrases

1. gremlin: *n.* an imaginary creature that people blame when a machine suddenly stops working（据说引起机械故障的）小精灵

2. electron: *n.* a very small piece of matter with a negative electric charge, found in all atoms 电子

3. widget: *n.* a small box on a computer screen that delivers changing information, such as news items or weather reports, while the rest of the page remains the same 小部件

---

4. compile: *v.* to translate instructions from one computer language into another so that a particular computer can understand them 编译

5. cursor: *n.* a small mark on a computer screen that can be moved and that shows the position on the screen where, for example, text will be added 光标

6. peripheral: *n.* a piece of equipment that is connected to a computer 外围设备

1. According to the video, how did the older mouses detect motion and distance?

A. With lights and sensors.

B. With a hard rubber ball and some plastic wheels.

C. Both A and B.

2. Which of the following instructions is NOT mentioned to be fetched and executed by the CPU?

A. Instructions to provide a way for the computer to interact with its environment.

B. Instructions to run the clock widget on your desktop.

C. Instructions to manage the files you're editing on the hard drive.

3. The simple task of clicking your mouse means visiting _____.

A. one gremlin

B. a human-readable programming language, like Java, C++, or Python

C. peripherals, the basic input-output system, the CPU, programs, and memory

Science News

Task 4: Moves and Details

Directions: Listen to a short piece of science news about *A Computer Algorithm that Can Gauge Relationships* and fill up blanks for each move.

New Words & Phrases

1. algorithm: *n.* a set of rules that must be followed when solving a particular problem 算法
2. gauge: *v.* to make a judgement about something, especially people's feelings or attitudes 判断
3. spouse: *n.* a husband or wife 配偶
4. acoustic: *adj.* related to sound or to the sense of hearing 声音的
5. warble: *n.* a high singing voice, especially one that is not very steady 颤音
6. psychological: *adj.* connected with a person's mind and the way in which it works 心理的，精神的
7. entail: *v.* to involve something that cannot be avoided 使必要
8. dynamics: *n.* the way in which people or things behave and react to each other in a particular situation（人或事物）相互作用的方式

Moves	Details
Finding	It turns out your tone really isn't what you say—it's how you say it. At least when it comes to couples in couples 1. c_____.
Method	Researchers developed a computer algorithm to gauge relationships between spouses based on their 2. v_____ patterns. The recordings were divided by acoustic features that used speech processing techniques to track pitch and voice warble and intensity.
	Example: Clips from the researcher's training video illustrate psychological states that characterize 3. d_____ relationships.
	The counseling sessions were also tested against 4. b_____ analyses with codes for positives such as "acceptance" and the negatives such as "blame".
Implication	One could imagine the algorithms may also work the same way when looking at 5. p_____ vocal patterns. Because even married couples sometimes say nice things to each other.

Task 5: News Retelling

Directions: Work with your partner and retell the news based on the moves in the table.

Part 3

Lecture

Task 6: Listening Comprehension

Directions: Watch part of a lecture entitled *Introduction to Computer Science and Programming* and answer the following three types of questions.

Basic Comprehension Questions

1. According to Alan Turing, how many primitive instructions were there?

_____

Pragmatic Understanding Questions

2. What is the purpose of mentioning Alan Turing?

_____

3. What does the professor imply when he says "this has its good side and its bad side"?

_____

Connecting Information Questions

4. Why does the author talk about a good chef?

_____

5. How does the author prove that "the computer will always do exactly what you tell them to do" is remarkable?

_____

Task 7: Lecture Structure

Directions: Watch the video again and fill in the lecture notes.

Interpreter:

An interpreter is a program that can execute any legal set of 1. i_____. And consequently, can be used to describe and accomplish anything you can do with a computer.

What a stored program computer looks like?

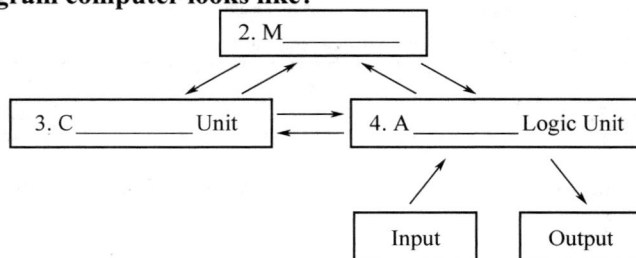

2. M_____

3. C_____ Unit   4. A_____ Logic Unit

Input   Output

Using a small set of instructions, you can build any kind of program you want:

- Typically, the computers have a very 5. s_____ number of built-in instructions. By combining those instructions in very clever ways, you can do 6. a_____ complex things.
- Alan Turing showed that there were six 7. p_____ instructions.

Each of which operated on one bit of information.

What instructions will you be using?

A 8. p_____ language provides a set of primitive instructions. A set of primitive control structures. So instructions and mechanisms for controlling the order in which they get executed.

What distinguishes one programming language from another?

- Instructions.
- Flow of 9. c_____.
- 10. C_____ mechanisms.

In fact, it's the combining mechanisms more than anything else that separate one language from another.

The most amazing thing about programming is that the computer will always do exactly what you tell them to do.

Part 4

Speech

Task 8: Speech Organization

Directions: Watch a TED talk entitled *The Self-assembling Computer Chips of the Future* and answer the following questions.

> **New Words & Phrases**
>
> 1. semiconductor: *n.* a solid substance that conducts electricity in particular conditions, better than insulators but not as well as conductors 半导体
>
> 2. quantum: *n.* a very small quantity of electromagnetic energy 量子
>
> 3. etch: *v.* to cut lines into a piece of glass, metal, etc. in order to make words or a picture 蚀刻
>
> 4. molecular: *adj.* relating to molecules (= groups of atoms that cannot be divided without a change in the chemical nature of the substance they are part of) 分子的
>
> 5. polymer: *n.* a substance consisting of large molecules (= groups of atoms) that are made from combinations of small simple molecules［高分子］聚合物
>
> 6. cylinder: *n.* a solid or hollow figure with round ends and long straight sides 圆柱体

➤ **Topic Introduction-Problem**
1. Now computers fit in our pocket, on our wrist and can even be implanted inside of our body. What enabled this?

_____

2. What does the speaker mean by "digital roadblock"?

_____

➤ **Topic Development**
Topic Development-Cause
3. The semiconductor industry is very well aware of the problem. What sorts of creative solutions are they working on? What disadvantage of them is mentioned?

_____

4. Why is the rate of miniaturization of transistors slowing down?

_____

5. As the transistor features get smaller and smaller, why are people seriously questioning: "Is this approach long-term viable?"

_____

Topic Development-Solution

6. What solution is provided by the speaker?

_____

7. What is the self-assemble material mentioned by the speaker called?

_____

8. Why does the speaker say that "the ability to self-assemble these structures only takes us half of the way"?

_____

9. What is the challenge with directed self-assembly?

_____

➢ **Topic Termination**

10. What is the speaker's attitude towards the future development of directed self-assembly?

_____

Task 9: Speech Outline

Directions: Please design a mind map in the box with your group and show the clear structure of this speech. You may refer to the questions in Task 8.

Task 10: Language Use

Directions: Watch the following clips of this video again and discuss the following questions with your partner.

Clip 1(00:12-01:04)
1. How does the speaker introduce his topic?

_____

Clip 2(02:34-03:46)
2. Why are human hair and red blood cell mentioned?

_____

Clip 3(06:23-06: 47)

3. How does the speaker explain that the solution of self-assembly can be robust?

_____

Clip 4 (06:48-07:16)

4. Why does the speaker mention his teenage son and daughter?

_____

Clip 5(07:48-09:00)

5. How does the speaker explain that "we can use molecular engineering to design different shapes of different sizes and of different periodicities"?

_____

Task 11: Discussion

Directions: Analyze the delivery skills of this speech and discuss with your partners. You may refer to the following points.

1. The speaker's body

(1) Personal appearance

(2) Eye contact

(3) Body movement

2. The speaker's voice

(1) Volume

(2) Rate

(3) Pauses

(4) Vocal variety

3. Visual aids

(1) Objects and models

(2) PowerPoint

Part 5

Oral Practice

Task 12: Group Presentation

Directions: Make a presentation on the topic of computer science with your group. The rest of students fill out the following evaluation form.

Presentation Evaluation Form

Items	5-Excellent	4-Good	3-Average	2-Fair	1-Poor
Topic Introduction					
Topic Development					
Topic Termination					
Language Use					
Delivery					
Overall Evaluation					

Unit 2

Wireless Communications

Science ABC

Task 1: Dictation

Directions: Listen to a recording entitled *What Is 5G and When Can We Get It* and complete the excerpt with one word in each blank.

> **New Words & Phrases**
> 1. cellular: *adj.* connected with a phone system that works by radio instead of wires（无线电话）蜂窝状的
> 2. transmission: *n.* the act or process of sending out an electronic signal or message or of broadcasting a radio or television programme 传送
> 3. fibre: *n.* a material such as cloth or rope that is made from a mass of natural or artificial threads 纤维
> 4. latency: *n.* the delay before data begins to move after it has been sent an instruction to do so 延迟
> 5. hazardous: *adj.* involving risk or danger, especially to somebody's health or safety 危险的

They say 5G is going to completely change our lives—from as simple as gaming, to driving, to as complex as medical care. This shift will be a once-in-a-decade 1. _____ for our wireless systems. Now, that all sounds great but what is it and when can I get it? Well, there's a brand-new second-generation cellular module from the current leading chip company, Qualcomm that 2. _____ the almighty power of 5G speeds for your phone except we all don't exactly have 5G phones yet, nor a 5G mobile network. However, this might be the year all of that changes. If you are just being brought up to speed, 5G is known as the fifth generation of wireless network communication.

Every time the technical rules that 3. _____ the inner workings of cellular networks changes, we get a new "generation," or "G" of technology, meaning to reap the 4. _____ people have to buy whole new phones, and carriers will need to install new transmission equipment to deliver the speeds they promised. When we got 1G it was for voice calls only, but then 2G gave us text messages, 3G added that 5. _____ support that we can't imagine being without, like vidchats and faster speeds, and now we have 4G—which has all the features of 3G but an added bump of speeds from 14 Mbps to 100Mbps which changed the game. Now we have video chats in HD, HD mobile TV, and live streamed apps, but this next one is gonna be big. 5G is 6. _____ to give users the fastest connectivity they've ever experienced. It's thought to be so fast it'd 7. _____ with our current fibre optic cables we have in our homes, and about ten to a hundred times faster than the phone you currently have in your hand.

But other than the major benefits of downloading "8K" videos in seconds, and using VR and AR seamlessly (goodbye buffering), why does the world want data coming in so fast? Well, 5G 8. _____ promises reduced latency, or lag time, to practically zero, meaning devices can communicate with each other in nearly real-time. We're talking about major improvements in the 9. _____ in devices that use sensors to make important decisions, like self-driving cars that need to suddenly brake, or industrial robots that can be sent to hazardous areas and be controlled 10. _____ from anywhere in the world, or better yet, anything in the healthcare field, from telemedicine, precision surgical robots, to remote surgery, or even virtual physical therapy sessions. All of this without any data slow down.

Task 2: True or False

Directions: Listen to a recording entitled *SmartHalo the Bike Navigator* and decide if the following statements are true or false. Write down T for True and F for False.

New Words & Phrases
1. inclined: *adj.* tending to do something; likely to do something 有……倾向
2. visual: *adj.* of or connected with seeing or sight 视觉的
3. awesome: *adj.* (especially North American English, informal) very good, great fun, etc.很好的

1. Knowing how to ride equals riding on a busy street easily and safely. _____
2. The less people check their smart phones, the safer the riding will be. _____
3. With SmartHalo, riders don't need to take out their smart phones frequently. _____
4. SmartHalo can't be removed from the bike, even with a special key. _____
5. SmartHalo developers intend to expand their device to bikes across the world. _____

Task 3: Multiple Choices

Directions: Watch a video entitled *Internet Services Provided by Starlink and the Cost* and choose the best answer.

New Words & Phrases
1. geosynchronous: *adj.* (of a satellite) moving around the earth at the equator at the same speed as the earth turns, so that it appears to be always in the same place in the sky（卫星）与地球旋转同步的
2. downside: *n.* the disadvantages or less positive aspects of something 不利的方面
3. proximity: *n.* the state of being near somebody/something in distance or time 接近
4. constellation: *n.* a group of stars that forms a shape in the sky and has a name 星座
5. repercussion: *n.* an indirect and usually bad result of an action or event that may happen some time afterwards 后果，不良影响

6. hype: *n.* advertisements and discussion in the media telling the public about a product and about how good or important it is 炒作，促销

7. troubleshoot: *v.* to analyse and solve serious problems for a company or other organization 解决重大问题

1. Why are Starlink's Internet speeds faster than those of previous Internet service providers?

A. The Starlink dishes connect to geosychronous satellites.

B. The Starlink satellites fly in low orbits.

C. Signals from the Starlink satellites are delayed.

2. Which of the following is not listed as a barrier for Starlink Internet users?

A. Professions.

B. Cost.

C. Technical support.

3. What is the main reason why the Nia Bay community needs better Internet?

A. The weather in the community is unpredictable.

B. Other Internet providers can't provide good services.

C. There aren't many opportunities for the locals.

Part 2

Science News

Task 4: Moves and Details

Directions: Listen to a short piece of science news entitled *Rectennas Convert Wi-Fi Signals into DC Electricity* and fill up blanks for each move.

New Words & Phrases
1. ubiquitous: *adj.* seeming to be everywhere or in several places at the same time; very common 普遍存在的
2. rectenna: *n.* a rectenna is a rectifying antenna, a special type of antenna that is used to convert microwave energy into direct current electricity 整流天线
3. rectifier: *n.* an electronic device that converts an alternating current to a direct current by suppression or inversion of alternate half cycles 整流器
4. microwatt: *n.* one millionth of a watt 微瓦特
5. biosensor: *n.* a device which uses a living organism or biological molecules to detect the presence of chemicals 生物传感器
6. stud: *v.* to dot or cover (with) 点缀

Moves	Details
Rationale	A big drawback of wearing a smartwatch is you often have to take it off to 1. c_____ it.
Findings	A device called a 2.r_____ is designed to capture energy from Wi-Fi signals and turn it into direct current electricity.
Methods	A small gold antenna converts a variety of 3.w_____ signals into an AC signal. Next, a rectifier changes that AC signal into usable DC electricity.
Results	The device is flexible, and, using typical Wi-Fi signals, it spits out about 40 microwatts, enough to light up a simple LED 4.d_____ or power a biosensor.
Implication	A smart city is envisioned where tiny 5.s_____ are ubiquitous, so it never goes dark.

Task 5: News Retelling

Directions: Work with your partners and retell the news based on the moves in the table.

Lecture

> ### New Words & Phrases
>
> 1. protocol: *n.* [countable] *(computing)* a set of rules that control the way data is sent between computers （计算机间交换信息的）协议
>
> 2. biometric: *adj.* using measurements of human features, such as fingers or eyes, in order to identify people 生物计量的
>
> 3. propagation: *n. (formal)* the act of spreading ideas, beliefs or information among many people 传送
>
> 4. megabit: *n.* a unit of computer memory or data, equal to 10^6, or $1,000^2$ (=1,000,000) bits 兆位
>
> 5. gigabit: *n.* a unit of computer memory or data, equal to 10^9, or $1,000^3$ (= 1,000,000,000)bits 吉位

Task 6: Listening Comprehension

Directions: Watch part of a lecture entitled *IoT Wireless Networks* and answer the following three types of questions.

Basic Comprehension Questions

1. What is this lecture mainly about?

_____

Pragmatic Understanding Questions

2. Why does the lecturer mention the case of a heart attack?

_____

3. How does the lecturer illustrate his point that "your Local Area Network is larger than your Personal Area Network"?

_____

Connecting Information Questions

4. How does the lecturer organize the information he presents to the audience?

_____

5. How does the lecturer explain "IEEE 802.11 standards"?

_____

Task 7: Lecture Structure

Directions: Watch the video again and fill in the lecture notes.

IoT Wireless Networks:

IoT Network Architecture

- A wireless PAN network is a small area network trying to enable wireless 1. c_____ of objects within something.
- A wireless LAN network is larger and may incorporate the 2. r_____ of a couple of personal area networks.

Wearable IoT Networks

- Wearable devices can be used to detect 3. b_____ information from sensors and IoT modules in our shoes, watch, etc.
- Smart devices collect information from the wearable devices and communicate with the control center and 4. m_____ server through the Internet.

Wi-Fi

- Wi-Fi devices include the smartphones, smart devices, 5. l_____ computers, PCs, etc.
- Application areas include homes, schools, computer 6. l_____, office buildings, etc.
- Wi-Fi devices and Access Points have a wireless communication range of about 30 meters 7. i_____.
- Wi-Fi data rates are based upon 8. p_____ type.

Bluetooth

- Bluetooth replaces 9. c_____ connecting many different types of devices.
- Bluetooth's standard PAN range is usually 10 meters.
- Bluetooth Low Energy provides reduced power 10. c_____ and cost.

Speech

Task 8: Speech Organization

Directions: Watch a TED talk entitled *Wireless Wake-up Call* and answer the following questions.

New Words & Phrases

1. meter: *n. (especially in compounds)* a device that measures and records the amount of electricity, gas, water, etc. that you have used or the time and distance you have travelled, etc. 表

2. insomnia: *n.* the condition of being unable to sleep 失眠

3. rendition: *n. [countable]* the performance of something, especially a song or piece of music; the particular way in which it is performed 表演

4. exponential: *adj. (formal)* (of a rate of increase) becoming faster and faster 快速增长的

5. ratchet up: to increase, or make something increase, repeatedly and by small amounts 稳步提高

6. carcinogenic: *adj.* likely to cause cancer 致癌的

➤ **Topic Introduction**
1. How does the presenter call the audience's attention to his topic?

_____

➤ **Topic Development**
Topic Development-Health Effects
2. What benefits has Internet brought to us according to the presenter?

_____

3. What were the symptoms of health effects of wireless technology on the presenter?

_____

4. How have some people's lives been changed by wireless technology?

_____

5. Why does the presenter say that all people are affected by wireless technology?

_____

6. What did the study by doctor Henry Lai indicate?

_____

Topic Development-Solutions
7. What can the wireless industry do to protect people and move the industry forward?

_____

8. How can we use our cell phones wisely according to the presenter?

_____

9. What is the presenter's advice on ensuring better sleep at night?

_____

> **Topic Termination**

10. How does the presenter end his speech?

_____

Task 9: Speech Outline

Directions: Please design a mind map in the box with your group and show the clear structure of this speech. You may refer to the questions in Task 8.

Task 10: Language Use

Directions: Watch the following clips of this video again and discuss the following questions with your partners.

Clip 1 (00:00-02:15)

1. How does the speaker highlight the fact that technology has rapidly increased in our lives?

_____

Clip 2 (02:16-04:26)

2. How does the speaker convince the audience that he is only one of the victims of wireless technology?

_____

Clip 3 (04:27-06:14)

3. How does the speaker vividly describe how hard it is for him to find a place to live?

_____

Clip 4 (06:55-09:24)

4. Why does the speaker mention EMF research and the World Health Organization?

_____

Clip 5 (09:25-10:23)

5. Why does the speaker mention the Federal Communications Commission?

_____

Task 11: Discussion

Directions: Analyze the delivery skills of this speech and discuss with your partners. You may refer to the following points.

1. The speaker's body

(1) Personal appearance

(2) Eye contact

(3) Body movement

2. The speaker's voice

(1) Volume

(2) Rate

(3) Pauses

(4) Vocal variety

3. Visual aids

(1) Objects and models

(2) PowerPoint

Part 5

Oral Practice

Task 12: Group Presentation

Directions: Make a presentation on the topic of health effects of wireless technology with your group. The rest of students fill out the following evaluation form.

Presentation Evaluation Form

Items	5-Excellent	4-Good	3-Average	2-Fair	1-Poor
Topic Introduction					
Topic Development					
Topic Termination					
Language Use					
Delivery					
Overall Evaluation					

Unit 3

Satellite Navigation

Science ABC

Task 1: Dictation

Directions: Listen to a recording entitled *How does GPS work* and complete the excerpt with one word in each blank.

New Words & Phrases

1. triangulate: *v.* determine (a height, distance, or location) by the use of triangles with a known base length and base angles 用三角测量法测定（高度、距离、方位等）

2. atomic: *adj.* relating to the energy that is produced when atoms are split; related to weapons that use this energy 原子的

3. relativity: *n.* Einstein's theory of the universe based on the principle that all movement is relative and that time is a fourth dimension related to space 相对论

4. detonation: *n.* an explosion; the action of making something explode 爆炸

We take navigation for granted these days. GPS receivers guide airplanes, cars, and even cell phones. But did you know that the Global Positioning System is 1. ＿＿＿＿＿＿ a big clock in space?

There are thirty GPS satellites in orbit, and they just 2. ＿＿＿＿＿＿ where they are and what time it is. All your phone GPS has to do is receive 3. ＿＿＿＿＿＿ from four satellites and it can triangulate its location in the four 4. ＿＿＿＿＿＿ in which we live, three space and one time.

But actually, it's not that simple. In order for navigation to work, the satellites carry atomic clocks 5. ＿＿＿＿＿＿ to the nanosecond, otherwise your GPS receiver might tell you you're halfway across town when you're still in the driveway. And special relativity tells us that moving clocks run slowly, while general relativity tells us that clocks run faster higher in a 6. ＿＿＿＿＿＿ field. These effects don't quite cancel, general relativity wins out and time indeed runs faster up in orbit with the satellites.

But some of the engineers working on the first GPS satellite couldn't bring themselves to believe that their clock would actually run fast just from being higher up, so they sent it up uncorrected. Within minutes it was off by enough to 7. ＿＿＿＿＿＿ GPS navigation, and by the end of the day, GPS receivers would have been wrong by tens of kilometers. Needless to say, the engineers turned the correction back on, and these days they trust general relativity.

Oh, and one last thing — GPS is also a nuclear weapons 8. ＿＿＿＿＿＿: there are always at least four GPS satellites 9. ＿＿＿＿＿＿ from any point on earth, and because of this, any nuclear detonation will be seen by enough satellites to 10. ＿＿＿＿＿＿ exactly where and when it took place.

Task 2: True or False

Directions: Listen to a recording entitled *How is China's BDS different from other global navigation networks* and decide if the following statements are true or false. Write down T for True and F for False.

New Words & Phrases

1. a bundle: a large amount of money 一大笔钱

2. Geostationary Earth Orbit: a circular orbit 35,785 km (22,236 miles) above earth's equator in which a satellite's orbital period is equal to earth's rotation period of 23 hours and 56 minutes 地球同步轨道

3. layout: *n.* the way in which the parts of something such as the page of a book, a website, a garden or a building are arranged 布局

4. distress: *n.* a situation in which a ship, plane, etc. is in danger or difficulty and needs help 遇险

---

1. Russia is one of the countries in the world with its own global navigation network. _____

2. The other navigation satellite systems have 24 satellites in low earth orbit. _____

3. Similar to GPS, GLONASS and Galileo, the BDS constellation has a relatively fixed range of activity. _____

4. BDS' accuracy in China and the Asia-Pacific region can be confined to 10 meters. _____

5. BDS service is unavailable in uninhabited areas such as deserts, forests, and mountainous or polar regions. _____

Task 3: Multiple Choices

Directions: Watch a video entitled *How smart is China's answer to GPS* and choose the best answer.

New Words & Phrases

1. Northern Celestial Hemisphere: part of a rotating astronomical region in the sky 北半天球

2. compatible: *adj.* (of machines, especially computers) able to be used together 兼容的

3. relief: *n.* food, money, medicine, etc. that is given to help people in places where there has been a war or natural disaster 救济

4. livestock husbandry: a branch of agriculture in which animal farming is carried out 畜牧业

5. herdsman: *n.* a person whose job is to take care of a group of animals such as sheep or cows in the countryside 牧民

---

1. How was "Big Dipper" used in ancient China as mentioned in the video?

A. People used it to know the time.

B. People used it for navigation.

C. Herdsmen used it to control their livestock.

2. Why was BeiDou Systems(BDS) updated?

A. To be compatible with GPS, GLONASS and Galileo.

B. To reduce the cost.

C. To achieve global coverage.

3. Which service does the remote-controlled water supply system rely on?

A. Short-messaging service.

B. Mobile communication network service.

C. Automatic driving service.

Science News

Task 4: Moves and Details

Directions: Listen to a short piece of science news entitled *Having an Albatross around Your Boat* and fill up blanks for each move.

New Words & Phrases
1. albatross: *n.* a very large white bird with long wings that lives in the Pacific and Southern Oceans 信天翁
2. emanate from: to come from something or somewhere 从……发出
3. glean: *v.* to obtain information, knowledge etc., sometimes with difficulty and often from various different places 四处收集
4. discrepancy: *n.* a difference between two or more things that should be the same 差异

Moves	Details
Finding	Albatrosses' behavior of following in 1. w_____ is used to track illegal fishing boats.
Method	Researchers attach data 2.l_____ to the backs of 169 albatrosses. The devices include a GPS and were able to detect the 3.p_____ and intensity of radar signals emanating from boats. So the researchers could track the location of the birds—and thus the radar-emitting boats—in real time.
Reason	Some vehicles deliberately switch off their 3. A_____ Identification Systems—something researchers say probably happens in illegal fishing operations.
Result	Birds could be an effective 5.boat-m_____ tool—as long as illegal fishing operations don't target them. However, the risk posed to albatross populations can still be underestimated.

Task 5: News Retelling

Directions: Work with your partners and retell the news based on the moves in the table.

Part 3

Lecture

New Words & Phrases

1. centrifugal: *adj.* moving or tending to move away from a center 离心的

2. angular velocity: the vector measure of the rotation rate, which refers to how fast an object rotates or revolves relative to another point 角速度

3. ITU: *n.* International Telecommunication Union 国际电信联盟

4. transponder: *n.* a device that receives a radio signal and then sends out a different signal in reply （发射机）应答器，转发器

5. gigahertz: *n.* a unit for measuring radio waves and the speed at which a computer operates; 1, 000, 000, 000 hertz 千兆赫

Task 6: Listening Comprehension

Directions: Watch part of a lecture entitled *How do satellites work* and answer the following three types of questions.

Basic Comprehension Questions

1. What is this lecture mainly about?

_____

2. How is the orbit chosen for placing the satellite?

_____

Pragmatic Understanding Questions

3. What does the speaker imply when he says "there are almost 4900 satellites orbiting the earth"?

_____

Connecting Information Questions

4. Why does the speaker say that "the geostationary belt is so crowded with satellites"?

_____

5. How does the professor introduce the "thrusters" as a component of satellites?

_____

Task 7: Lecture Structure

Directions: Watch the video again and fill in the lecture notes.

How do satellites work?

- Current situation: There are almost 1._____ satellites orbiting the earth our planet every day.
- Why are satellites in totally different orbits?
  - ✓ Principle: Satellite stays in orbit because of the 2. b_____ between gravitational pull and centrifugal force.
  - ✓ LEO: The closest to the earth at an 3. a_____ of between 160 and 2000 kilometers. It is chosen by satellites built for the earth observation, weather 4. f_____, geographic area surveying, satellite phone calls, etc.
  - ✓ GEO: The ideal choice for television broadcasting since you do not have to 5. a_____ the angle of your satellite dish again and again.
  - ✓ MIO: The wise option for navigation 6. a_____ such as GPS.
- What are the main components of communication satellites?
  - ✓ Transponders: To change the frequency of the received signal, remove any signal noise and 7. a_____ the signal power.
  - ✓ Batteries and solar panels: To power the electronic equipment. But during an 8. e_____ time, the batteries are used.
  - ✓ Thrusters: To transfer inactive satellites to the 9. g_____ orbit.
- What are the main components of GPS satellites?
  - ✓ The most important components are an atomic clock and the 10. a_____.

Part 4

Speech

Task 8: Speech Organization

Directions: Watch a TED talk entitled *Let's clean up the space junk orbiting earth* and answer the following questions.

New Words & Phrases

1. propellant: *n.* a gas that forces out the contents of an aerosol 推进剂，喷射剂

2. errand: *n.* a job that you do for somebody that involves going somewhere to take a message, to buy something, deliver goods, etc.任务，使命，差事

3. stutter: *v.* (of a vehicle or an engine) to move or start with difficulty, making short sharp noises or movements 吃力地运行

4. dubious: *adj.* not certain about something and suspecting that something may be wrong; not knowing whether something is good or bad 可疑的

➤ **Topic Introduction-Problem**

1. How does the presenter introduce the topic?

_____

➤ **Topic Development**

Topic Development-Cause

2. What is the problem brought by our reliance on satellites?

_____

3. How do we deal with satellites that are no longer working currently?

_____

4. What is the trend of satellite-launching in the future?

_____

5. What is "the graveyard"?

_____

6. What are the problems with national and international efforts to deal with space debris and junk?

_____

Topic Development-Solution

7. Which aspects does the speaker propose to solve the problem?

_____

8. How is TechDemoSat-1 designed as an encouraging sign?

_____

9. What is the problem existing in our way of exploring the space?

_____

➢ **Topic Termination**
10. How does the speaker end her speech?

_____

Task 9: Speech Outline

Directions: Please design a mind map in the box with your group and show the clear structure of this speech. You may refer to the questions in Task 8.

```
┌──────────────────────────────────────────────────────────────────────┐
│                                                                        │
│                                                                        │
│                                                                        │
│                                                                        │
│                                                                        │
│                                                                        │
└──────────────────────────────────────────────────────────────────────┘
```

Task 10: Language Use

Directions: Watch the following clips of this video again and discuss the following questions with your partners.

Clip 1(00:00-00:32)
1. How does the speaker draw out the subject of the speech?

_____

Clip 2(01:11-02:15)
2. How does the speaker explain the harm brought by space junks?

_____

Clip 3(02:34-03: 01)
3. Why does the author mention the world's first satellite Sputnik I?

_____

Clip 4(05:23-06:16)
4. Why does the speaker raise the question "What if we were smarter about how we designed satellites?

_____

Clip 5(06:16-06:47)

5. Why does the speaker mention UK's TechDemoSat-1?

_____

Task 11: Discussion

Directions: Analyze the delivery skills of this speech and discuss with your partners. You may refer to the following points.

1. The speaker's body

(1) Personal appearance

(2) Eye contact

(3) Body movement

2. The speaker's voice

(1) Volume

(2) Rate

(3) Pauses

(4) Vocal variety

3. Visual aids

(1) Objects and models

(2) PowerPoint

Part 5

Oral Practice

Task 12: Group Presentation

Directions: Make a presentation on the topic of the influence of Starlink with your group. The rest of students fill out the following evaluation form.

Presentation Evaluation Form

Items	5-Excellent	4-Good	3-Average	2-Fair	1-Poor
Topic Introduction					
Topic Development					
Topic Termination					
Language Use					
Delivery					
Overall Evaluation					

Unit 4

Internet of Things

Science ABC

Task 1: Dictation

Directions: Listen to a recording entitled *We Need to Prepare for the Internet of Things* and complete the excerpt with one word in each blank.

New Words & Phrases

1. appliance: *n.* a machine that is designed to do a particular thing in the home, such as preparing food, heating or cleaning（家用）电器

2. seamless: *adj.* happening without any sudden interruption or difficulty 无缝的

3. replenish: *v.* to make something full again by replacing what has been used 补充

4. obstacle: *n.* a situation, an event, etc. that makes it difficult for you to do or achieve something 障碍

5. unforeseen: *adj.* not expected 未预见到的

6. unintended: *adj.* not intended 无意的

A top technology analyst has 1. _____ that the world might not yet be ready for what is called the Internet of Things. This is the next stage of the digital and technological 2. _____. It will greatly 3. _____ our lives via the interconnectedness of all the devices, services, and appliances we use in our daily life. The technology research company Gartner predicts that nearly 4. _____ devices will be on the Internet of Things. All of these things will communicate with each other to make even simple decisions, like ordering a new carton of milk, a seamless experience. The fridge will simply contact the 5. _____ service when it senses stocks need 6. _____.

The Computer World magazine says that while the Internet of Things has, "the potential to 7. _____ fundamental economic and social change," there are "serious obstacles" to ensuring the 8. _____ of this technological revolution is in place in time. These include the building of new data storage centers, data storage and management, and data security. Gib Sorebo, a cybersecurity expert, warns of the unforeseen. He says "the law of unintended consequences" on the Internet could 9. _____ problems with the explosion in the number of connected devices. He predicts that 10. _____ will become a primary concern because of the huge number of things in our daily life that will be connected to the Internet.

Task 2: True or False

Directions: Listen to a recording entitled *Smart Cities* and decide if the following statements are true or false. Write down T for True and F for False.

New Words & Phrases

1. telepresence: *n.* the use of various technologies to operate equipment from a different place 远程操控

2. mastermind: *n.* an intelligent person who plans and directs a complicated project or activity 策划者，决策者

3. congestion: *n.* the state of being crowded and full of traffic（交通）拥塞

4. sustainable: *adj.* causing little or no damage to the environment and therefore able to continue for a long time 可持续的

5. asset: *n.* a useful or valuable thing or person 有价值的事物或有益的人，资产

1. Smart cities are just science fiction now. _____

2. A built-in "telepresence" system allows users to turn on the heating. _____

3. About 75% of the world's population is expected to live in cities by 2050. _____

4. IBM has designed a system to ease traffic congestion. _____

5. According to Dan Hill, the most important thing in smart cities is to make cities perform better. _____

Task 3: Multiple Choices

Directions: Watch a video entitled *What Is the Internet of Things* and choose the best answer.

New Words & Phrases

1. a myriad of: a great number of 大量的

2. augment: *v.* to increase the amount, value, size, etc. of something 增强

3. bombard: *v.* to attack somebody with a lot of questions, criticisms, etc. or by giving them too much information 大量提问，大肆抨击，提供过多信息

4. optical: *adj.* using light for reading or storing information 光存储的

5. quantify: *v.* to describe or express sth. as an amount or a number 量化

1. What processes all our questions and commands?

A. The smart speaker.

B. Cloud service.

C. The security camera.

2. Which of the following is less useful to the speaker?

A. Turning on and off the lights.

B. Storing his lighting preferences.

C. Bombarding him with ads.

3. The Internet of Things understands our behavior, NOT by _____.

A. collecting and analyzing data

B. quantifying every aspect of our lives

C. figuring out the reason of our behavior

Science News

Task 4: Moves and Details

Directions: Listen to a short piece of science news entitled *Pro Baseball Player Tech Avatars Could Be a Hit* and fill up blanks for each move.

New Words & Phrases

1. Hall of Famer: a person who is inducted to the Hall of Fame 名人堂成员

2. hitter: *n.* a person in baseball who hits the ball 击球手

3. stroke: *n.* an act of hitting a ball when playing a sport 击球

4. pitch: *n.* a throw in a baseball game 投球

5. swing: *n.* a stroke delivered with a sweeping arm movement 挥动

6. knob: *n.* handle 把手

7. accelerometer: *n.* an instrument for measuring acceleration 加速度计

8. gyroscope: *n.* a device containing a wheel that spins rapidly inside a frame and does not change position when the frame is moved 陀螺仪，回转仪

9. avatar: *n.* an incarnation in human form 虚拟化身

10. batter: *n.* a hitter 击球手

11. never want to mince words: to say sth. in a direct way even though it might offend other people 直言不讳

12. pitcher: *n.* the player who throws the ball to the batter 投球手

13. quote unquote: a phrase used to place verbal quotation marks around the following word, usually to convey scepticism about the validity or truth of that phrase 用于口头表达时，表示对所引用的词或短语加上引号，以表示讽刺、怀疑或不赞同的态度,相当于中文中的"所谓"

Moves	Details
Orientation	According to Ted Williams, the hardest thing to do in sports is 1. _____. So, some professional baseball players are turning to science to improve their multimillion-dollar 2. _____ .
Rationale	Some approaches focus on the neuroscience of hitting. But for more info about the 3. _____ itself, Zepp Labs makes a "Smart Bat".
Findings	The sensor in the knob of the "Smart Bat" measures bat speed, hand speed, 4. _____ and other factors, and sends this info to a smartphone app. The app then uses this data to 5. _____ the swing, in the hope that the batter can make the necessary 6. _____.
Future work	Maybe somebody could come up with a 7. _____ to help the pitchers.

Task 5: News Retelling

Directions: Work with your partners and retell the news based on the moves in the table.

Part 3

Lecture

New Words & Phrases

1. instantiate: *v.* to represent or be an example of something 实例化，具现化
2. deploy: *v.* to use sth. effectively 有效利用
3. vendor: *n.* a company that sells a particular product 销售公司
4. authenticate: *v.* to prove that something is true 认证
5. segment: *v.* to divide sth. into different parts 分割
6. jostle: *v.* to push roughly 推、撞、挤

Task 6: Listening Comprehension

Directions: Watch part of a lecture entitled *Wired Networking Overview* and answer the following three types of questions.

Basic Comprehension Questions

1. What is this lecture mainly about?

_____

2. For designing networks, how do designers take devices and put them together?

_____

3. What is the result of having no very strongly accepted industry standards?

_____

Pragmatic Understanding Questions

4. What is the purpose of mentioning "software design" at the beginning of the lecture?

_____

Connecting Information Questions

5. How does the professor clarify the points he makes about IoT protocols?

_____

Task 7: Lecture Structure

Directions: Watch the video again and fill in the lecture notes.

Smart Home Design Architecture

Get Internet service:

- Have a 1. c_____ modem provided by an Internet service provider (ISP). ISPs run more
  2. s_____ protocols such as DOCSIS.
- Or have a DSL modem for phone line communications.

Inside your home:

- Have an IoT Hub to 3. c_____ the various segmented smart devices in your home for 4. s_____ reasons and 5. m_____ reasons.
- Your IoT Hub will
  - ✓ speak Wi-Fi to your Wi-Fi access 6. p_____,
  - ✓ then speak a specialized 7. p_____ to these individual devices.

Challenges:

- Too many different protocols that are
  - ✓ not really 8. c_____ with each other,
  - ✓ not very well 9. d_____.
- Security
  - ✓ 87% of devices are 10. v_____ at this point in time.

Speech

Task 8: Speech Organization

Directions: Watch a TED talk entitled *Are Smart Devices Helping or Harming Us* and answer the following questions.

New Words & Phrases

1. paleo diet: a nutritional approach that focuses on eating only foods that are high in nutrients, unprocessed, and based on the foods that were available and eaten by humans in Paleolithic times 原始人饮食法

2. spam email: advertising email that people who have not asked for it 垃圾邮件

3. drain: *v.* to cause the gradual disappearance of 耗尽

4. Fitbit: *n.* a wearable fitness tech that tracks your vital signs and measures steps, distance, calories burned, active minutes and sleep 智能手环

5. default: *n.* what happens or appears if you do not make any other choice or change 默认值

6. integrate: *v.* to mix with or join a society or a group of people 融入

7. breach: *v.* to make an opening, especially in order to attack someone or something behind it 入侵

8. data breach: an incident in which secure, sensitive, and confidential information is accessed and exposed to an unauthorized and untrusted environment 数据外泄

9. epidemic: *n.* a sudden rapid increase in how often sth. bad happens 蔓延

10. data trafficking: illegal trade in data 数据非法交易

11. revenue: *n.* money receives from a business 收益

12. opt: *v.* to choose to take or not to take a particular course of action 选择

13. chopping block: a steady wooden block on which food can be cut or diced 砧板

14. fib: *n.* a lie about sth. that is not important 小谎

> **Topic Introduction-Problem**

1. How does the speaker introduce her topic?

_____

> **Topic Development**

Topic Development-Cause

2. What is the definition of the Internet of Things device?

_____

3. What might happen if a hacker can gain access to just one of your Internet of Things devices?

_____

4. What do we know about the speaker?

_____

5. What does the speaker mean by saying "data is the new oil"?

_____

6. What is our thinking error, according to the speaker?

_____

Topic Development-Solution
7. Why is the speaker's risk management dream world not realistic?

_____

8. What is the general guideline on whether or not to trust a company or a device?

_____

9. What actions can we take to protect ourselves?

_____

➤ **Topic Termination**
10. How does the speaker end her speech?

_____

Task 9: Speech Outline

Directions: Please design a mind map in the box with your group and show the clear structure of this speech. You may refer to the questions in Task 8.

```



```

Task 10: Language Use

Directions: Watch the following clips of this video again and discuss the following questions with your partners.

Clip 1 (01:09-01:28)
1. How does the speaker establish the relationship between her topic and the audience?

_____

Clip 2 (02:02-02:46)

2. How does the speaker move from the advantages to the problems of IoT devices?

_____

Clip 3 (06:24-07:19)

3. How does the speaker show that our private information could become public?

_____

Clip 4 (11:15-11:20)

4. Why does the speaker admit that she told a lie earlier?

_____

Clip 5 (11:20-11:42)

5. How does the speaker end her speech?

_____

Task 11: Discussion

Directions: Analyze the delivery skills of this speech and discuss with your partners. You may refer to the following points.

1. The speaker's body

(1) Personal appearance

(2) Eye contact

(3) Body movement

2. The speaker's voice

(1) Volume

(2) Rate

(3) Pauses

(4) Vocal variety

3. Visual aids

(1) Objects and models

(2) PowerPoint

Part 5

Oral Practice

Task 12: Group Presentation

Directions: Make a presentation on the topic of IoT with your group. The rest of students fill out the following evaluation form.

Presentation Evaluation Form

Items	5-Excellent	4-Good	3-Average	2-Fair	1-Poor
Topic Introduction					
Topic Development					
Topic Termination					
Language Use					
Delivery					
Overall Evaluation					

Unit 5

Artificial Intelligence

Part 1

Science ABC

Task 1: Dictation

Directions: Listen to a recording entitled *What is AI* and complete the excerpt with one word in each blank.

New Words & Phrases

1. augmented: *adj.* having been made greater in size or value 扩大了的，增加了的

2. consciousness: *n.* the fact of awareness by the mind of itself and the world 意识

3. implement: *v.* put (a decision, plan, agreement, etc.) into effect 贯彻，实行，履行（决定、计划、协议等）

4. ethical: *adj.* of or relating to moral principles or the branch of knowledge dealing with these （与）道德（有关）的，（与）伦理（有关）的

Distributed computing and IoT have led to massive amounts of data, and social networking has encouraged most of that data to be unstructured. We want experts to scale their 1.c_____ and let the machines do the time-consuming work.

How do we define intelligence? Human beings have innate intelligence, defined as the intelligence that 2. g_____ every activity in our body. This intelligence is what causes an oak tree to grow out of a little seed, and an elephant to form from a single-celled organism.

[Weak AI]

Weak or Narrow AI is AI that is applied to a specific domain. For example, language translators, virtual assistants, self-driving cars, 3. AI-_____ web searches, recommendation engines, and intelligent spam filters. Applied AI can perform specific tasks, but not learn new ones, making decisions based on programmed 4. a_____, and training data.

[Strong AI]

Strong AI or Generalized AI is AI that can 5. i_____ and operate a wide variety of independent and unrelated tasks. Generalized intelligence is the 6. c_____ of many AI strategies that learn from experience and can perform at a human level of intelligence.

[Super AI]

Super AI or Conscious AI is AI with human-level consciousness, which would require it to be 7. s_____.

[Summary]

AI is the fusion of many fields of study. Computer science and electrical engineering determine how AI is 8. i_____ in software and hardware. Mathematics and statistics determine viable models and measure performance. Because AI is modeled on how we believe the brain works, psychology and linguistics play an 9. e_____ role in understanding how AI might work. And philosophy provides guidance on intelligence and 10. e_____ considerations.

Task 2: True or False

Directions: Listen to a recording entitled *Steven Hawking's prediction on AI* and decide if the following statements are true or false. Write down T for True and F for False.

> **New Words & Phrases**
>
> 1. launch: *n.* an occasion at which a new product or publication is introduced to the public（新产品，出版物）发布会，推介会
> 2. spell: *v.* lead to 导致，招致

1. The development of artificial intelligence means the end of the human race. _____

2. Steven Hawking has been dependent on technology to communicate. _____

3. The new system had been life-changing for Steven Hawking and had the potential to greatly improve the lives of disabled people all over the world. _____

4. Professor Hawking warns that AI could spell the end of the human race if fully developed. _____

5. We hope that technology can solve all humanity's problems rather than threatening its existence. _____

Task 3: Multiple Choices

Directions: Watch a video entitled *AI is here* and choose the best answer.

> **New Words & Phrases**
>
> 1. oceanography: *n.* the branch of science that deals with the physical and biological properties and phenomena of the sea 海洋学
> 2. optimistic: *adj.* hopeful and confident about the future 乐观的，乐观主义的
> 3. pessimistic: *adj.* lacking in hope and confidence in the future 悲观的
> 4. corny: *adj.* showing no new ideas or too often repeated, and therefore not funny or interesting 陈腐的，俗套的

1. Which represents the third wave of Industrial Revolution?

A. Steam engine

B. Electricity

C. Computer

2. What is the AI they are talking about?

A. Smart cellphone

B. Autonomous objects

C. Powerful computer

3. Which is not mentioned about AI's benefits for mankind?

A. Transportation and oceanography

B. Poverty alleviation and cybersecurity

C. Education and healthcare

Science News

Task 4: Moves and Details

Directions: Listen to a short piece of science news entitled *Tech's Brain Effect: It's Complicated* and fill up blanks for each move.

New Words & Phrases
1. adolescent: *n.* a juvenile between the onset of puberty and maturity 青少年
2. well-being: the state of being comfortable, healthy, or happy 舒适，健康，幸福
3. lump: *v.* put in an indiscriminate mass or group; treat as alike without regard for particulars 混为一谈，（不顾具体情况的差异而）同等看待
4. variable: *n.* an element, feature, or factor that is liable to vary or changing 可变性，可变因素，变量

Moves	Details
Background	There's been a lot of mostly negative hype around this issue, often referred to as screen time, and how it's 1. r_____ all of our lives. …, the truth is that everything we 2. e_____ changes our brains.
Findings	In fact, a recent study examining over 350,000 adolescents found a small but negative 3. a_____ with technology use and well-being, but they also found 4. s_____ relationships between eating potatoes and wearing eyeglasses and well-being.
Purpose	Part of the issue in studying how technology influences our brain is that there are so many different forms of technology that often all get lumped into one 5. c_____. So, how we use technology, what specific technology we use, and what we use it for will be important 6. v_____ to define in future research.
Results	And even as we do more and better research on these topics, the answer is still likely to be that it's 7. c_____.
Explanation	In a way, we're all part of a massive experiment in how technology is influencing our brains, and there will almost certainly be both positive and negative 8. o_____.
Methods	So, studies that 9. t_____ individuals' behavioral and brain development over time will be particularly important. Like the ABCD, or Adolescent Brain and Cognitive Development Study, which is currently following over 10,000 kids for 10 years.
Implication	And this kind of research will be especially important in helping us to figure out what 10. l_____ influences technology has on our brains.

Task 5: News Retelling

Directions: Work with your partners and retell the news based on the moves in the table.

Lecture

New Words & Phrases

1. undeniable: *adj.* unable to be denied or disputed 不可否认的，无可争辩的

2. variation: *n.* a different or distinct form or version of something 变化，变异

3. Claude Shannon(1916-2001): American mathematician and electrical engineer who laid the theoretical foundations for digital circuits and information theory, a mathematical communication model 克劳德·香农

4. ingredient: *n.* a component part or element of something 组成部分或元素

5. undistinguishable: *adj.* not clearly recognizable or understandable 难区分的，不可分辨的

6. recipe: *n.* a set of instructions for making something from various ingredients 食谱

7. explicit: *adj.* leaving no question as to meaning or intent 明晰的，明确的

8. implicit: *adj.* present but not consciously held or recognized 隐性的，暗含的

9. scalable: *adj.* capable of being easily expanded or upgraded on demand 可扩展的，可升级的

10. script: *n.* (computing) a sequence of instructions or commands for a computer to execute, esp. one that automates a small task (such as assembling or sorting a set of data) 脚本文件

Task 6: Listening Comprehension

Directions: Watch part of a lecture entitled *Artificial Intelligence* and answer the following three types of questions.

Basic Comprehension Questions

1. What aspects of AI is this lecture mainly discussing?

_____

2. What are the three basic ingredients to building an AI?

_____

Pragmatic Understanding Questions

3. What is the purpose of mentioning the American Si-Fi movie "AI"?

_____

Connecting Information Questions

4. How does the professor clarify the points he makes about Neural Networks?

_____

5. How does the professor clarify the points he makes about Deep Learning algorithms?

Task 7: Lecture Structure

Directions: Watch the video again and fill in the lecture notes.

Artificial Intelligence

1. Underlying Trend
   - The main algorithm used by Deep Blue was actually a 1. v_____ of an approach described by the mathematician Claude Shannon in 1950.
   - The kind of artificial intelligence displayed by Deep Blue was possible, thanks to the massive increase in 2. p_____ power.

2. Definition
   - AI is a system that is able to 3. e_____traits of human intelligence like reasoning, learning from experience or interacting with humans in natural language.
   - General AI is typically what you see in the movies, a complete system that is 4. i_____ from a human. It knows or can learn anything humans can learn, has 5. e_____, even has a purpose in life.
   - Narrow AI is less 6. a_____. It is when a system exhibits human-like intelligence traits on a specific field or task.

3. What are those algorithms that allow us to build intelligent machines
   - Machine learning: e. g., we need to write algorithms capable of looking at thousands of bird pictures and 7. i_____ from that some implicit way to recognize a bird.
   - Neural Networks: the algorithm takes the input data, let's say a picture, feeds it into artificial 8. n_____ that work together to recognize, for example, that there is a Shama bird in the picture.
   - Deep Learning: e.g., to 9. e_____ arrival time for millions of Uber rides based on city traffic history, or come up with accurate sentence translation by learning from all the web pages out there that are available in multiple languages. The field of research is a 10. p____ one.

Speech

Task 8: Speech Organization

Directions: Watch a TED talk entitled *How to get empowered, not overpowered, by AI* and answer the following questions.

New Words & Phrases

1. cochlear implants: an electronic device that is put into the inner ear during an operation in order to allow severely deaf people to hear some sounds 人工耳蜗

2. chauvinism: *n.* exaggerated or aggressive patriotism; excessive or prejudiced support or loyalty for one's own cause, group, or sex 沙文主义

3. backflip: *n.* a backward somersault done in the air with the arms and legs stretched out straight. 后空翻

4. waterfront: *n.* a part of a town that borders a body of water 滨海区，滨湖区，滨河区

5. luddite: *n.* one who is opposed to especially technological change 守旧的人

6. scaremongering: *n.* the action of spreading stories that make people feel worried or frightened 危言耸听

7. lousy: *adj.* very bad 糟糕的，差劲的

8. holy grail: something that a person or a particular group of people want very much to have or achieve 圣杯，终极的宝物

9. inception: *n.* the beginning of an organization or official activity 开始，开端

10. complacent: *adj.* feeling so satisfied with your own abilities or situation that you feel you do not need to try any harder 沾沾自喜的，自鸣得意的

11. obsolete: *adj.* not in use any more, having been replaced by something newer and better or more fashionable 过时的，废弃的

12. envision: *v.* to imagine or expect something to happen, appear, etc. in a particular way 想象，预想

13. flounder: *v.* struggle or stagger helplessly or clumsily in mud or water （在泥或水中）无助（或笨拙）地挣扎、蹒跚

14. proactive: *adj.* (of a person, policy, or action) creating or controlling a situation by causing something to happen rather than responding to it after it has happened （人、政策、行为）引发性的，积极的，主动的

15. mitigate: *v.* make less severe, serious, or painful 使温和，使缓和，减轻（痛苦）

16. stigmatize: *v.* describe or regard as worthy of disgrace or great disapproval 指责，把……污蔑为

---

17. qualm: *n.* an uneasy feeling of doubt, worry, or fear, especially about one's own conduct; a misgiving 疑惧，疑虑，担忧

> **Topic Introduction-Problem**

1. How does the presenter introduce his topic?

_____

> **Topic Development**

Topic Development-Cause

2. What are the basic steps of realizing AI development for humanity?

_____

3. Why does the presenter use the abstract landscape of tasks?

_____

4. What is AGI?

_____

5. How soon are we going to get AGI?

_____

6. What do we want the role of humans to be if machines can do everything better and cheaper than us?

_____

Topic Development-Solution

7. What is the best strategy to deal with AGI?

_____

8. What has to be included in AI safety work? And why?

_____

9. What is the gist of "friendly AI"?

_____

> **Topic Termination**

10. How does the presenter end his speech?

_____

Task 9: Speech Outline

Directions: Please design a mind map in the box with your group and show the clear structure of this speech. You may refer to the questions in Task 8.

Task 10: Language Use

Directions: Watch the following clips of this video again and discuss the following questions with your partner.

Clip 1 (01:30-02:25)
1. Why does the speaker use Apollo 11 moon mission as an example at the beginning?

_____

Clip 2 (02:45-03:54)
2. How does the speaker explain the amazing power of AI to the audience?

_____

Clip 3 (04:00-04:51)
3. Why did the audience laugh when the speaker mentioned "the obvious takeaway is to avoid careers at the waterfront" while talking about the AI landscape of tasks?

_____

Clip 4 (07:22-08:18)
4. How does the speaker prove the old strategy of learning from mistakes lousy?

_____

Clip 5 (10:15-11:29)
5. Why does the speaker ask the audience to raise their hand if their computer has ever crashed?

_____

Task 11: Discussion

Directions: Analyze the delivery skills of this speech and discuss with your partners. You may refer to the following points.

1. The speaker's body

(1) Personal appearance

(2) Eye contact

(3) Body movement

2. The speaker's voice

(1) Volume

(2) Rate

(3) Pauses

(4) Vocal variety

3. Visual aids

(1) Objects and models
(2) PowerPoint

Part 5

Oral Practice

Task 12: Group Presentation

Directions: Make a presentation on the topic of Artificial Intelligence with your group. The rest of students fill out the following evaluation form.

Presentation Evaluation Form

Items	5-Excellent	4-Good	3-Average	2-Fair	1-Poor
Topic Introduction					
Topic Development					
Topic Termination					
Language Use					
Delivery					
Overall Evaluation					

Unit  6

Blockchain

Science ABC

Task 1: Dictation

Directions: Listen to a recording entitled *What Is Blockchain* and complete the passage with one word in each blank.

New Words & Phrases

1. transparent: *adj.* allowing you to see through it 透明的

2. ecological: *adj.* connected with the relation of plants and living creatures to each other and to their environment 生态的

3. tamper (with): *v.* to make changes to something without permission, especially in order to damage it 篡改

4. decentralize: *v.* to give some of the power of a central government, organization, etc. to smaller parts or organizations around the country 去中心化

5. peer-to-peer: *adj.* (of a computer system) in which each computer can act as a server for the others, allowing data to be shared without the need for a central server 点对点的

6. leapfrog: *v.* jump across 跨越，超越

7. scalability: *n.* the fact that it is possible to adapt something to meet greater needs in the future 可扩展性

8. consensus: *n.* an opinion that all members of a group agree with 共识，一致性

What is blockchain? The blockchain is a public blockchain, a blockchain system that is not controlled by any person or 1. _____ where it allows everyone to have the same right to speak and read the data on the chain, so that the information is 2. _____ . The blockchain promotes the ecological development of the main net through the original set of un-tampering 3. _____ mechanisms. At the same time, the blockchain can also protect the rights and interests of all users in the system. It is a highly secure and highly 4. _____ peer-to-peer network. The blockchain is a 5. _____ that can support many application scenarios, such as finance, assets, 6. _____ , management, proof of rights, Internet of Things, supply chain, and other 7. _____ applications. In addition, the blockchain has leapfrogged 8. _____ in many fields such as security, trust, 9. _____ , and scalability of application scenarios. And it is a blockchain public network that is truly built by a 10. _____ .

Task 2: True or False

Directions: Listen to a recording entitled *What Is Bitcoin Mining* and decide if the following statements are true or false. Write down T for True and F for False.

New Words & Phrases

1. distribute: *v.* to give things to a large number of people; to share something between a number of people 分发

2. issue: *v.* officially give something 分发

3. currency: *n.* the system of money that a country uses 货币

4. transaction: *n.* a piece of business that is done between people, especially an act of buying or selling 交易

5. processor: *n.* (*computing*) a part of a computer that controls all the other parts of the system 处理器

6. graphics card: a circuit board that allows a computer to show images on its screen 显卡

7. chip: *n.* electronic equipment consisting of a small crystal of a silicon semiconductor fabricated to carry out a number of electronic functions in an integrated circuit 芯片

8. integrated: *adj.* in which many different parts are closely connected and work successfully together 集成的

9. circuit: *n.* an electrical device that provides a path for electrical current to flow 电路

10. pool: *n.* a group of people available for work when needed 矿池（区块链技术专用词）

11. proportionate: *adj.* increasing or decreasing in size, amount or degree according to changes in something else 成比例的

---

1. In Bitcoin mining, the more the miners, the less secure the network. _____

2. The inventor of Bitcoin will change the difficulty of the math problems in terms of the speed problems are being solved. _____

3. The chips are faster than graphics cards, and also power-saving. _____

4. Miners often work together to solve the math problems. _____

5. Mining is very important to keep the fairness and security of the Bitcoin network. _____

Task 3: Multiple Choices

Directions: Watch a video entitled *How Does a Blockchain Work* and choose the best answer.

New Words & Phrases

1. timestamp: *v./n.* (make) a mark or record that shows when something happened, especially a digital record of when something was done in a computer or other electronic system （盖）时间戳

2. notary: *n.* a person, especially a lawyer, with official authority to be a witness when somebody signs a document and to make this document legally acceptable 公证人

---

3. cryptocurrency: *n.* any system of electronic money, used for buying and selling online and without the need for a central bank 数字货币

4. ledger: *n.* a book or electronic document in which a bank, a business, etc. records the money it has paid and received 账本

5. hash: *n.* an encoding of data into a small, fixed size; used in hash tables and cryptography 散列（函数）

6. genesis: *n.* the beginning or origin of something 起源

7. proof-of-work: *n.* a form of cryptographic proof in which one party (the prover) proves to others (the verifiers) that a certain amount of a specific computational effort has been expended 工作量证明

8. entity: *n.* something that exists separately from other things and has its own identity 实体

9. node: *n.* (*computing*) a piece of equipment such as a computer, that is attached to a network 节点

10. smart contract: a computer protocol that facilitate, verify, or enforce the negotiation or performance of a contract 智能合约

11. JavaScript: *n.* a programming language that is one of the core technologies of the World Wide Web 基于对象和事件驱动的客户端脚本语言

1. What information is contained in a block?

A. A timestamp, data of the block, and the hash of the block.

B. Data of the block, data of the previous block, and the hash of the block.

C. Data of the block, the hash of the block, and the hash of the previous block.

2. Why is a hash compared to a fingerprint?

A. Because the hash of a block has a timestamp.

B. Because the hash of a block cannot be changed.

C. Because the hash of a block is always unique.

3. Why is the genesis block special?

A. Because it cannot be tempered with.

B. Because it cannot point to previous blocks.

C. Because it has no hash.

4. What mechanisms ensure the security of a blockchain according to the video?

A. Timestamp, use of hashing, proof-of-work mechanism.

B. Use of hashing, proof-of-work mechanism, being distributed.

C. being distributed, notary, proof-of-work mechanism.

5. Which of the following statement is true?

A. Smart contracts can automatically exchange coins based on certain conditions.

B. To successfully tamper with a blockchain, you'll need to take control of all the peer-to-peer network.

C. The technique of blockchain was originally described by Satoshi Nakamoto.

Science News

Task 4: Moves and Details

Directions: Listen to a short piece of science news entitled *Cyber Currencies Get Boost from High-profile Endorsements* and fill up blanks for each move.

New Words & Phrases
1. on the ropes: (informal) very close to being defeated 濒于失败，处于困境
2. preeminent: *adj.* more important, more successful or of a higher standard than others 卓越的
3. ilk: *n.* type; kind 种类，同类
4. coinage: *n.* the coins used in a particular place or at a particular time; coins of a particular type 货币
5. subscriber: *n.* a person who pays money, usually once a year, to receive regular copies of a magazine or newspaper or have access to it online 用户，订购者
6. rapper: *n.* a person who speaks the words of a rap song 说唱歌手
7. album: *n.* a collection of pieces of music released as a single item, usually on the Internet or on a CD 专辑
8. catchy: *adj.* attractive, pleasant 吸引人的
9. high-profile: *adj.* receiving or involving a lot of attention and discussion in the media 高调的
10. endorsement: *n.* a public statement or action showing that you support somebody/something 宣传，代言
11. token: *n.* a round piece of metal or plastic used instead of money to operate some machines or as a form of payment 代币

Moves		Details
Statement		Despite its heavy decline in value earlier this year, the fate of Bitcoin have recently 1. r_____.
Development 1- Exemplification		Apple will allow the use of certain cyber 2. c_____.
Development 2- Exemplification		Some satellite TV 3. s_____ will pay their monthly bills using Bitcoin.
Development 3- Exemplification		Music lovers can use Bitcoin to pay for the latest 4. a_____ of rapper 50 Cent.
Claim		Such 5. h_____ endorsements will boost Bitcoin, but its value may fall once more people buy it.

Task 5: News Retelling

Directions: Work with your partners and retell the news based on the moves in the table.

Lecture

New Words & Phrases

1. demo: *n.* an act of showing or explaining how something works or is done 演示

2. SHA: *n.* short for Secure Hash Algorithm 安全散列算法

3. character: *n.* a letter, sign, mark or symbol used in writing, in printing or on computers 字符

4. nonce: *n.* an arbitrary number that can be used just once in a cryptographic communication 随机数

5. arbitrarily: *adv.* in a way that does not seem to be based on a reason, system or plan and sometimes seems unfair 任意地

6. fake: *adj.* (disapproving) not what somebody claims it is; appearing to be something it is not 假的

7. mutation: *n.* a change in the form or structure of something 改变

Task 6: Listening Comprehension

Directions: Watch part of a lecture entitled *Blockchain Demo* and answer the following three types of questions.

Basic Comprehension Questions

1. What is this lecture mainly about?

_____

2. Why does the professor say that the hash which begins with four zeros is relatively unusual?

_____

Pragmatic Understanding Questions

3. At the end of the video, what does the professor try to indicate by bothering himself to go far back to Block 2 and make a change, and then mine Block 3, 4, and 5?

_____

Connecting Information Questions

4. How does the professor clarify "hash"?

_____

5. How does the professor clarify "nonce"?

_____

Task 7: Lecture Structure

Directions: Watch the video again and fill in the lecture notes.

Blockchain Demo:

What is hash?

- It looks like a bunch of 1. r _____ numbers.
- It's a digital 2. f_____ of data.
- Hash will be exactly the same as long as you put exactly the same 3. i _____ in.

What is a block?

- A block consists of:
  - ✓ some kind of 4. n_____,
  - ✓ a 5. n_____,
  - ✓ some 6. d_____.
- Nonce is a 7. n_____ that you set so that the hash starts with many zeros.

What is a blockchain?

- The hash of each block points to the hash in the 8. p_____ block.
- The change of information in a block will 9. i_____ the block.
- A blockchain can 10. r_____ mutation.

Part 4

Speech

Task 8: Speech Organization

Directions: Watch a TED talk entitled *How the Blockchain Will Radically Transform the Economy* and answer the following questions.

New Words & Phrases

1. bribery: *n.* the giving or taking of bribes 贿赂

2. grease: *n.* any thick oily substance, especially one that is used to make machines run smoothly 润滑油

3. hunter-gatherer: *n.* a member of a group of people who do not live in one place but move around and live by hunting, fishing and gathering plants 狩猎采集的人

4. recourse: *n.* the right of someone who holds a bill of exchange that is not paid when it becomes due to claim payment from people who have signed the bill 追索权

5. attestation: *n.* the evidence 证明

6. cobble (something together): *v.* to produce something quickly and without great care or effort, so that it can be used but is not perfect 草率地拼凑

7. attribute: *n.* a quality or feature as belonging to somebody/something 特质

8. sign off on: (*informal*) to express your approval of something formally and definitely 赞同

9. monopoly: *n.* (*business*) the complete control of trade in particular goods or the supply of a particular service 垄断

10. token: *n.* a unique identifier of an interaction session 令牌

11. renege: *v.* to break a promise, an agreement, etc. 违背（承诺、保证等）

12. enforcer: *n.* a person whose responsibility is to make sure that other people perform the actions they are supposed to, especially in a government 实施者，强制执行者

13. escrow: *n.* a contractual arrangement in which a third party receives and disburses money or property for the primary transacting parties 暂由第三方保管

14. collateralize: *v.* pledge as a collateral 以……作抵押

15. intervention: *n.* action taken to improve or help a situation 干预

16. floor: *v.* to surprise or confuse somebody so that they are not sure what to say or do 使惊讶得不知所措

17. harness: *v.* to control and use the force or strength of something to produce power or to achieve something 利用

---

18. counterfeit: *adj.* made to look exactly like something in order to trick people into thinking that they are getting the real thing 假冒的

19. start-up: *n.* a company that is just beginning to operate 初创企业

> **Topic Introduction-Announce Topic**

1. How does the speaker introduce her topic?

_____

> **Topic Development**

Topic Development-Introduce History

2. In human history, how did people find ways to lower uncertainties about one another and be able to do trade?

_____

Topic Development-Definition and Expansion

3. What is the blockchain?

_____

4. Why is the blockchain closest in description to something like Wikipedia?

_____

Topic Development-Solution

5. What are the three forms of uncertainty that we face in almost all of our everyday transactions where blockchains can play a role?

_____

6. How do blockchains lower the first uncertainty?

_____

7. How do blockchains lower the second uncertainty?

_____

8. How do blockchains lower the third uncertainty?

_____

Topic Development-Weakness and Benefits

9. What are the weaknesses of the blockchain, and what benefits has it brought to us?

_____

> **Topic Termination**

10. How does the speaker end her speech?

_____

Task 9: Speech Outline

Directions: Please design a mind map in the box with your group and show the clear structure of this speech. You may refer to the questions in Task 8.

Task 10: Language Use

Directions: Watch the following clips of this video again and discuss the following questions with your partners.

Clip 1 (00:00-00:33)

1. Why does the speaker mention legal systems, corporations, marketplaces?

_____

Clip 2 (00:34-01:00)

2. Why does the speaker begin her speech by telling the history of institutions?

_____

Clip 3 (03:13-03:58)

3. How does the speaker explain to the audience what is the blockchain?

_____

Clip 4 (03:59-05:22)

4. What's the purpose of the speaker when she compares the blockchain to Wikipedia?

_____

Clip 5 (05:57-07:29)

5. What's the purpose of the speaker when she uses an example to clarify the first uncertainty we face in almost all of our everyday transactions, that is, not knowing who we're dealing with?

_____

Task 11: Discussion

Directions: Analyze the delivery skills of this speech and discuss with your partners. You may refer to the following points.

1. The speaker's body

(1) Personal appearance

(2) Eye contact

(3) Body movement

2. The speaker's voice

(1) Volume

(2) Rate

(3) Pauses

(4) Vocal variety

3. Visual aids

(1) Objects and models

(2) PowerPoint

Part 5

Oral Practice

Task 12: Group Presentation

Directions: Make a presentation on the topic of blockchain with your group. The rest of students fill out the following evaluation form.

Presentation Evaluation Form

Items	5-Excellent	4-Good	3-Average	2-Fair	1-Poor
Topic Introduction					
Topic Development					
Topic Termination					
Language Use					
Delivery					
Overall Evaluation					

Unit

Big Data

Science ABC

Task 1: Dictation

Directions: Listen to a recording entitled *Big Data—the Development* and complete the excerpt with one word in each space.

New Words & Phrases

1. elusive: *adj.* difficult to find, define or achieve 难以捉摸

2. voluminous: *adj.* (of a container, piece of furniture, etc.) very large 非常庞大的

3. wrangle: *n.* an argument that is complicated and continues over a long period of time（长时间的）争论，争吵

4. fledgling: *n.* (usually before another noun) a person, an organization or a system that is new and without experience 初出茅庐的人

5. terabyte: *n.* a unit of computer memory or data, equal to 2^{40} (= 1 099 511 627 776) bytes 太字节

6. outstrip: *v.* to become larger, more important, etc. than somebody/something 比……大（或重要等），超过

7. orchestrate: *v.* to organize a complicated plan or event very carefully or secretly 精心安排，策划，密谋

Big data is an elusive concept. It represents an amount of digital information, which is uncomfortable to store, transport, or analyze. Big data is so voluminous that it 1. _____ the technologies of the day and challenges us to create the next generation of data storage tools and techniques. So, big data isn't new.... Fifty years ago, CERN's data could be stored in a single computer. OK, so it wasn't your usual computer, this was a 2. _____ computer that filled an entire building. To analyze the data, physicists from around the world traveled to CERN to connect to the 3. _____ machine.

In the 1970's, our ever-growing big data was distributed across different sets of computers, which mushroomed at CERN. Each set was joined together in 4. _____, homegrown networks....

In the 1980's, islands of similar networks speaking different dialects 5. _____ all over Europe and the States, making remote access possible but torturous. To make it easy for our physicists across the world to access the ever-expanding big data stored at CERN without traveling, the networks needed to be talking with the same language. We adopted the fledgling Internet working standard from the States, followed by the rest of Europe, and we established the 6. _____ link at CERN between Europe and the States in 1989, and the truly global Internet took off!

Physicists could easily then access the terabytes of big data remotely from around the world, 7. _____ results, and write papers in their home institutes. Then, they wanted to share their findings with all their colleagues. To make this information sharing easy, we created the web in the early 1990's....

During the early 2000's, the continued growth of our big data 8. _____ our capability to analyze it at CERN, despite having buildings full of computers.... In order to orchestrate these interconnected resources with their 9. _____ technologies, we developed a computing grid, enabling the seamless sharing of computing resources around the globe. This relies on trust relationships and mutual exchange. But this grid model could not be transferred out of our community so easily, where not everyone has resources to share nor could companies be expected to have the same level of trust. Instead, an alternative, more business-like approach for accessing on-demand resources has been 10. _____ recently, called cloud computing, which other communities are now exploiting to analyze their big data.

Task 2: True or False

Directions: Listen to a recording entitled *Big Data* and decide if the following statements are true or false. Write down T for True and F for False.

> **New Words & Phrases**
> 1. unravel: *v.* to explain sth. that is difficult to understand or is mysterious; to become clearer or easier to understand 阐释，说明
> 2. strand: *n.* one of the different parts of an idea, a plan, a story, etc. 部分，方面
> 3. leverage: *v.* to get as much advantage or profit as possible from sth. that you have 利用

1. Data now comes from many resources, such as computers, smartphones, bikes, TVs and even our watches and shoes. _____

2. If we gathered all the data from the beginning of time until the year 2000, it would be less than we now create in a second. _____

3. Big data changed people's viewpoints on the world. _____

4. Since the possible applications of big data are endless, businesses will be prosperous with big data. _____

5. Companies can turn to Advanced Performance Institute for help in understanding and leveraging big data. _____

Task 3: Multiple Choices

Directions: Watch a video entitled *Big Data in Five Minutes* and choose the best answer.

> **New Words & Phrases**
> 1. snap: *n.* a photograph, especially one taken quickly 快照

2. veracity: *n.* the quality of being true; the habit of telling the truth 真实性

3. churn rate: the number of people who stop using a product and change to another or who leave the company they work for and go to another 流失率

1. How many search queries are made per minute on the Google?

A. 2.1 million.

B. 4.5 million.

C. 3.8 million.

2. Which of the following does not belong to the five V's of big data?

A. All data is generated at a very high speed in the form of patient records and test results.

B. All data will enable faster disease detection, better treatment and reduced cost.

C. Approximately 40 exabytes of data gets generated every month by a single smartphone user.

3. Which of the following is not taken by Hadoop to store big data?

A. They will classify data into structured, semi-structured and unstructured data.

B. They will break down files into smaller chunks and store in various machines.

C. They will use a distributed file system to make sure data is safe even if one machine fails.

Part 2

Science News

Task 4: Moves and Details

Directions: Listen to a short piece of science news entitled *Data Reveals Most Influential Movies* and fill up blanks for each move.

<table>
<tr><td colspan="2" align="center">New Words & Phrases</td></tr>
<tr><td colspan="2">1. spoof: v. to copy a film, TV programme, etc. in a humorous way by exaggerating its main features 滑稽模仿，恶搞
2. flick: n. (old-fashioned, informal) a film 电影
3. shoot-em-up: n. a movie involving a lot of violence with guns 枪战片</td></tr>
</table>

Moves	Details
Findings	If you go by 1. t_____ sales, the most popular film of all time is *Gone With the Wind*. That is adjusting for 2.i_____.
Problem	But a movie's take at the box office is influenced by ad 3. b_____, distribution, reviews.
Method	To 4. a_____ that question, researchers gave movies the big data treatment, tracking and analyzing all factors that indicate a movie's influence on 5. s_____ films.
Result	And by 6. a_____ those connections with a handful of algorithms, the data scientists came up with a new number one—*The Wizard of Oz* .
Limitations	The analysis does have limitations. It favors older films, and the 7. u_____ IMDb data has been shown to be biased towards Western movies. That is, the products of western civilization, not shoot-em-ups.

Task 5: News Retelling

Directions: Work with your partners and retell the news based on the moves in the table.

Part 3

Lecture

New Words & Phrases

1. obscure: *v.* to make it difficult to see, hear or understand sth. 使模糊

2. dilemma: *n.* a situation which makes problems, often one in which you have to make a very difficult choice between things of equal importance（进退两难的）窘境，困境

3. coarsen: *v.* to become or make sth. become thicker and/or rougher（使）变厚，变粗糙

4. transcript: *n.* a written or printed copy of words that have been spoken 抄本，誊本

5. receipt: *n.* a piece of paper that shows that goods or services have been paid for 收据，收条

6. round off: to change an exact figure to the nearest whole number 四舍五入

7. substitute: *v.* to take the place of sb./sth. else; to use sb./sth. instead of sb./sth. else（以……）代替，取代

8. stakeholder: *n.* a person or company that is involved in a particular organization, project, system, etc., especially because they have invested money in it（某组织、工程、体系等的）参与人，参与方，有权益关系者

Task 6: Listening Comprehension

Directions: Watch part of a lecture entitled *Data Governance* and answer the following three types of questions.

Basic Comprehension Question

1. What do we mean by governance in the context of ML projects?

_____

Pragmatic Understanding Questions

2. What does the professor mean by saying we trade accuracy or sensitivity in the coarsening approach?

_____

3. What is the professor's attitude towards protecting sensitive data fields before making it available?

_____

Connecting Information Questions

4. How does the professor clarify "masking"?

_____

5. How does the professor explain that "Zip Three" works in the "Zip or postal codes" scenario in the coarsening approach?

_____

Task 7: Lecture Structure

Directions: Watch the video again and fill in the lecture notes.

Introduction:
What is governance?
- the ongoing practice of applying rules for protecting and 1. c_____ access to your data

In implementing ML use cases, balance data access against security implications of data access.
- train ML systems on a subset of the raw data or on the entire dataset after 2. o_____ the data
  - ✓ e.g., you might train an ML model that uses customer feedback on a product and protect the 3. p_____ of the people

Three goals for ML and privacy:
- 4. i_____ sensitive data
  - ✓ specific columns in structured datasets
  - ✓ unstructured text-based datasets that followed known patterns
  - ✓ free form unstructured data
    e.g., text reports, audio recordings, photographs or 5. s_____ receipts
  - ✓ combinations of fields
    We can 6. b_____ the last two digits of their zip code.
- protect sensitive data
  - ✓ you could remove, 7. m_____ or coarsen sensitive data.
  - ✓ fields particularly well-suited for the coarsening approach: GPS location, zip or postal codes, 8. n_____ quantities and IP addresses.
- create public governance documentation

Factors to consider when managing data in the Cloud for ML:
- data security
- 9. r_____ and compliance
- 10. v_____ and control

Speech

Task 8: Speech Organization

Directions: Watch a TED talk entitled *Big Data Is Better Data* and answer the following questions.

> **New Words & Phrases**
> 1. archaeologist: *n.* a person who studies archaeology 考古学家
> 2. spreadsheet: *n.* a computer program that is used, for example, when doing financial or project planning. You enter data in rows and columns and the program calculates costs, etc. from it（计算机）电子表格程序
> 3. enshrine: *v.* to make a law, right, etc. respected or official, especially by stating it in an important written document 把（法律、权利等）奉为神圣，把……庄严地载入
> 4. overtly: *adv.* in a way that is open and not secret 明显地
> 5. biopsy: *n.* the process of removing and examining tissue from the body of somebody who is ill, in order to find out more about their disease 活组织检查
> 6. criminology: *n.* the scientific study of crime and criminals 犯罪学

> ➤ **Topic Introduction-Announce Topic**
1. How does the speaker introduce his topic?

_____

> ➤ **Topic Development**

Topic Development-Present an Argument
2. What does the speaker say they find when they have a large body of data?

_____

Topic Development-Offer an Explanation
3. What is the difference between information in 4000 years ago and now?

_____

4. What shall we do to record Martin Luther's location in the 1500s?

_____

5. What are the effective uses of data when the speaker mentions the issue of posture?

_____

Topic Development-Advantages and Disadvantages
6. Which is one of the most impressive areas that can reflect the value of big data?

_____

7. Who is better when researchers looked at the question of cancerous biopsies, the machine or the people? And why?

_____

8. What are the dark sides to big data?

_____

9. What are the challenges in small data era and big data age respectively?

_____

➤ **Topic Termination**
10. What suggestions does the speaker give at the end of his speech?

_____

Task 9: Speech Outline

Directions: Please design a mind map in the box with your group and show the clear structure of this speech. You may refer to the questions in Task 8.

┌───┐
│   │
│   │
│   │
│   │
│   │
└───┘

Task 10: Language Use

Directions: Watch the following clips of this video again and discuss the following questions with your partners.

Clip 1(03:35-04:50)
1. How does the speaker clarify the difference between data from a clay disk discovered on the island of Crete to the disk used by us now?

_____

Clip 2(07:05-07:25)
2. How does the speaker account for driver fatigue function?

_____

Clip 3(07:41-08: 06)
3. How does the speaker explain what is machine learning?

_____

Clip 4 (08:09-11:22)

4. How does the speaker further clarify machine learning?

_____

Clip 5(12:54-13:17)

5. How does the speaker clarify that big data and algorithms are going to challenge the white collar?

_____

Task 11: Discussion

Directions: Analyze the delivery skills of this speech and discuss with your partners. You may refer to the following points.

1. The speaker's body

(1) Personal appearance

(2) Eye contact

(3) Body movement

2. The speaker's voice

(1) Volume

(2) Rate

(3) Pauses

(4) Vocal variety

3. Visual aids

(1) Objects and models

(2) PowerPoint

Part 5

Oral Practice

Task 12: Group Presentation

Directions: Make a presentation on the topic of big data with your group. The rest of students fill out the following evaluation form.

Presentation Evaluation Form

Items	5-Excellent	4-Good	3-Average	2-Fair	1-Poor
Topic Introduction					
Topic Development					
Topic Termination					
Language Use					
Delivery					
Overall Evaluation					

Unit 8

Quantum Computing

Science ABC

Task 1: Dictation

Directions: Listen to a recording entitled *Google Claims Major Breakthrough in Quantum Computing* and complete the excerpt with one word in each space.

New Words & Phrases
1. supremacy: *n.* power to dominate or defeat 霸权，优势
2. revolutionize: *v.* change sth. radically 彻底变革
3. binary: *adj.* consisting of two (units or components) or based on two 二进制的
4. qubit: *n.* a unit of quantum information 量子比特

Google says it has reached a major 1. _____ in quantum computing research. Scientists reported Wednesday in the 2. _____ *Nature* about successful experiments involving quantum technology. The team said that, in one test, its quantum computer 3. _____ was able to complete a complex 4. _____ problem in just 200 seconds. The same problem would have taken the world's fastest supercomputer 10,000 years to complete, the scientists said. Researchers described the new breakthrough as "quantum supremacy." This term describes a point at which a quantum computer can perform a 5. _____ that a traditional computer could never complete within its lifetime.

Quantum computing is a 6. _____ technology, it is designed to greatly 7. _____ the processing of information. Experts believe quantum computers could one day revolutionize many industries. Major technology companies besides Google are also working to develop the technology. They include Microsoft, IBM and Intel.

Traditional computers process information as a 8. _____ of bits. Each bit can be either a zero or a one in the binary language of computing. But quantum bits, known as qubits, can be both zero and one at the same time. These special 9. _____ can theoretically permit a quantum computer to perform calculations at far higher speeds than today's fastest supercomputers. Quantum computing could be useful in understanding complex areas of chemistry, 10. _____ and physics.

Task 2: True or False

Directions: Listen to a recording entitled *Quantum Computers: Computing the Impossible* and decide if the following statements are true or false. Write down T for True and F for False.

New Words & Phrases

1. mixture: *n.* a substance consisting of two or more substances mixed together 混合体
2. entangle: *v.* twist together or entwine into a confusing mass 纠缠
3. interference: *n.* electrical or acoustic activity that can disturb communication 干扰
4. entanglement: *n.* an intricate trap that entangles or ensnares its victim 纠缠
5. sweep: *n.* covering or extending over an area or time period 扫过
6. tackle: *v.* accept sth. as a challenge 应对
7. protein: *n.* a substance found in food and drink such as meat, eggs, and milk 蛋白质
8. encryption: *n.* the activity of converting from plain text into code 加密
9. scale up: 按比例增加
10. a trick up its sleeves: 锦囊妙计

1. Quantum computers are made of qubits instead of bits. _____

2. Qubits can be a mixture of 1 and 0 at the same time. _____

3. In normal computers, it's difficult to add more bits. _____

4. Too much interference from the outside might make the entanglement of qubits broken. _____

5. If scientists can one day build a powerful quantum computer, it probably would be useful for everyday tasks. _____

Task 3: Multiple Choices

Directions: Watch a video entitled *The High-stakes Race to Make Quantum Computers* and choose the best answer.

New Words & Phrases

1. superposition: *n.* the placement of one thing on top of another 叠加
2. sphere: *n.* the apparent surface of the imaginary sphere on which celestial bodies appear to be projected 球体
3. manipulate: *v.* hold something in one's hands and move it 操作
4. properties: *n.* a basic or essential attribute shared by all members of a class 性质
5. fragile: *adj.* easily broken or damaged or destroyed 脆弱的
6. fluctuation: *n.* the quality of being unsteady and subject to changes 波动
7. collision: *n.* a brief event in which two or more bodies come together 碰撞
8. elaborate: *adj.* developed or executed with care and in minute detail 复杂精细的
9. fickle: *adj.* liable to sudden unpredictable change 易变的
10. ion: *n.* a particle that is electrically charged (positive or negative) 离子
11. rotate: *v.* turn on or around an axis or a center 旋转
12. sub-atomic particles: 亚原子粒子，次原子粒子
13. stray electromagnetic fields: 杂散电磁场

1. In order to clarify the two states of one and zero, what does the speaker use to analogize the

two states?

A. A superposition.

B. Bits and qubits.

C. North and south poles on a sphere.

2. What is the advantage of a quantum computer with the growing complexity of problems?

A. It can calculate the solution faster than a classical computer.

B. It doesn't require more qubits to handle them.

C. It can switch back and forth between the states of one and zero.

3. Why do quantum computers need elaborate set-ups?

A. Because quantum states are vulnerable and might be easily destroyed by certain factors.

B. Because atomic and subatomic particles correspond to the state of the qubit.

C. Because we can only control a few qubits in the same place at the same time.

4. Which one of the following statements is TRUE?

A. To manage changeable quantum states effectively, we only need to know how a quantum computer controls its particles.

B. A trapped ion quantum computer uses ions to represent its fickle states with lasers.

C. At present, trapped ions and superconducting qubits are the two major approaches in managing the fickle quantum states effectively.

Science News

Task 4: Moves and Details

Directions: Listen to a short piece of science news entitled *Quantum Computing Is Attracting Commercial Interest* and fill up blanks for each move.

> **New Words & Phrases**
> 1. intuitive: *adj.* spontaneously derived from or prompted by a natural tendency 直觉的
> 2. conceivable: *adj.* capable of being imagined 可想象的
> 3. intractable: *adj.* difficult to manage or mold 棘手的
> 4. catalyst: *n.* (chemistry) a substance that initiates or accelerates a chemical reaction without itself being affected （化学）催化剂
> 5. juggle: *v.* manipulate 调控，操控
> 6. boon: *n.* a desirable state 益处
> 7. constraint: *n.* something that controls what you do by keeping you within particular limits 约束条件
> 8. consultancy: *n.* the agency giving expert advice within a particular field 咨询公司
> 9. ornery: *adj.* having a difficult and contrary disposition 低劣的
> 10. dub: *v.* give a nickname to 把……称为，给……起绰号
> 11. intermediate: *adj.* lying between two extremes in time or space or degree 中等程度的

Moves	Details
Statement	Big, stable quantum computers would be useful devices. They could perform some calculations faster than any 1. c_____ non-quantum machine.
Development	They would probably be much more rapid than any 2. c_____ computer at searching a database. They would be quicker at more specific tasks, too. They would also speed up the analysis of 3. o_____ problems.
Problem	Unfortunately, big, stable quantum computers do not yet exist.
Solution	But small, ornery, unstable ones, dubbed as NISQS do. Some see NISQS as mere stepping stones towards size and 4. s_____. A growing number of companies and 5. i_____, however, are hopeful that NISQS themselves will be able to do useful work in the meantime.

Task 5: News Retelling

Directions: Work with your partners and retell the news based on the moves in the table.

Part 3

Lecture

New Words & Phrases

1. module: *n.* a self-contained unit or item that is used along with other components 模块

2. astrophysics: *n.* the branch of astronomy concerned with the physical and chemical properties of celestial bodies 天体物理学

3. in a nutshell: summed up briefly 简而言之

4. nanometer: *n.* a metric unit of length equal to one billionth of a meter 纳米

5. diameter: *n.* a straight line connecting the center of a circle with two points on its perimeter 直径

6. shrink: *v.* reduce in size; reduce physically 缩小

7. magnetic: *adj.* of or relating to or caused by magnetism 磁性的

8. photon: *n.* a quantum of electromagnetic radiation; an elementary particle that is its own antiparticle 光子

9. polarization: *n.* the phenomenon in which waves of light or other radiation are restricted in direction of vibration 偏振

10. filter: *n.* an electrical device that alters the frequency spectrum of signals passing through it 滤波器

11. deduce: *v.* conclude by reasoning 推断

Task 6: Listening Comprehension

Directions: Watch part of a lecture entitled *Quantum Computers Explained: Limits of Human Technology* and answer the following three types of questions.

Basic Comprehension Questions

1. What is this lecture mainly about?

_____

2. Why does the speaker say that the most famous use of quantum computers is ruining IT security?

_____

Pragmatic Understanding Questions

3. At the end of the video, what does the speaker try to imply?

_____

Connecting Information Questions

4. How does the speaker illustrate "to use unusual quantum properties to their advantage"?

_____

5. How does the speaker explain "quantum computers are vastly superior in some areas"?

_____

Task 7: Lecture Structure

Directions: Watch the video again and fill in the lecture notes.

Limits of Human Technology or Not?

What is the problem?

- The power of our brain machines has kept growing 1. e_____, but this process is about to meet its physical limits.
  - ✓ As transistors are 2. s_____ to the size of only a few atoms, electronics may just 3. t_____ themselves to the other side of a blocked passage via a process called Quantum Tunneling.
- In the quantum 4. r_____, physics works quite differently from the predictable ways and traditional computers just stop making sense.

How to solve this problem?

- Scientists are trying to use the unusual quantum 5. p_____ to their advantage by building quantum computers.
  - ✓ 6. S_____ is a game changer. In the quantum world, the qubit doesn't have to be in just one of the states 1 and 0 but can be in any proportions of both states at once.
  - ✓ Qubit 7. m_____ is a mind bender as well. A normal logical gate gets a simple set of input and produces one definite output. A quantum gate manipulates an input of superpositions, 8. r_____ probabilities and produces another superposition as its output.

Is the solution effective/workable?

- Quantum computers will probably not replace our home computers, but they are vastly 9. s_____ in some areas.
  - ✓ One of them is database searching. The most famous use of quantum computers is ruining IT security.
  - ✓ Another really exciting new use is simulations. They could provide new insights on proteins that may 10. r_____ medicine.
- Right now, we don't know if quantum computers will be just a very specialized tool, or a big revolution for humanity.

Part 4

Speech

Task 8: Speech Organization

Directions: Watch a TED talk entitled *The Promise of Quantum Computers* and answer the following questions.

New Words & Phrases

1. sequence: *v.* arrange in a particular order 按序排列

2. genome: *n.* the full DNA sequence of an organism 基因组

3. paralysis: *n.* loss of the ability to move a body part 瘫痪

4. vaccine: *n.* immunogen consisting of a suspension of weakened or dead pathogenic cells injected in order to stimulate the production of antibodies 疫苗

5. minuscule: *adj.* very small 微不足道的

6. deterministically: *adv.* being an inevitable consequence of antecedent sufficient causes 确切地

7. probabilistically: *adv.* by the use of probability theory 有概率性地

8. revert: *v.* go back to a previous state 恢复

9. hallmark: *n.* a distinctive characteristic or attribute 特征

10. fuse: *v.* mix together different elements 结合

11. ammonia: *n.* a pungent gas compounded of nitrogen and hydrogen (NH3) 氨

12. expend: *v.* use up, consume fully 消耗

13. electrostatic: *adj.* concerned with or producing or caused by static electricity 静电的

14. nitrogenase: *n.* an enzyme of nitrogen-fixing microorganisms that catalyzes the conversion of nitrogen to ammonia 固氮酶

15. inhibitor: *n.* a substance that retards or stops an activity 抑制剂

16. discreet: *adj.* marked by prudence or modesty and wise self-restrain 谨慎的

17. stimulus: *n.* any stimulating information or event; acts to arouse action 促进因素

18. hurdle: *n.* an obstacle that you are expected to overcome 障碍

19. precipitous: *adj.* done with very great haste and without due deliberation 鲁莽的

20. defy: *v.* resist or confront with resistance 违抗

21. abacus: *n.* a calculator that performs arithmetic functions by manually sliding counters on rods or in grooves 算盘

22. clinical trials: 临床试验

23. pharmaceutical companies: 制药公司

➤ **Topic Introduction-Problem**

1. How does the speaker bring up the topic?

_____

2. What is the core problem of the topic?

_____

3. What might be the possible solution?

_____

➤ **Topic Development**

Topic Development-Working Mechanism

4. How does quantum computing work?

_____

Topic Development-Evaluation

5. Is there value to the so-called quantum speedups?

_____

6. Why should quantum computing be not just about triumphs in the lab?

_____

7. How long are we going to wait for quantum computing?

_____

Topic Development-Advice

8. What kind of attitude shall we take toward the quantum advantage?

_____

9. What's needed to prepare for the maturity of quantum computing?

_____

➤ **Topic Termination**

10. How does the speaker end the speech?

_____

Task 9: Speech Outline

Directions: Please design a mind map in the box with your group and show the clear structure of this speech. You may refer to the questions in Task 8.

Task 10: Language Use

Directions: Watch the following clips of this video again and discuss the following questions with your partners.

Clip 1 (00:54-01:43)

1. Why does the speaker mention the example of computational drug design?

_____

Clip 2 (00:30-02:56)

2. How does the speaker present the core problem of the topic?

_____

Clip 3 (02:56-04:22)

3. How does the speaker illustrate how quantum computers work?

_____

Clip 4 (04:22-07:35)

4. Why does speaker mention the cases of "fertilizer production" and "drug discovery"?

_____

Clip 5 (10:23-12:08)

5. What's the purpose of quoting the Nobel Prize winner and the facts of the government?

_____

Task 11: Discussion

Directions: Analyze the delivery skills of this speech and discuss with your partners. You may refer to the following points.

1. The speaker's body

(1) Personal appearance

(2) Eye contact

(3) Body movement

2. The speaker's voice

(1) Volume

(2) Rate

(3) Pauses

(4) Vocal variety

3. Visual aids

(1) Objects and models
(2) PowerPoint

Part 5

Oral Practice

Task 12: Group Presentation

Directions: Make a presentation on the topic of quantum computing with your group. The rest of students fill out the following evaluation form.

Presentation Evaluation Form

Items	5-Excellent	4-Good	3-Average	2-Fair	1-Poor
Topic Introduction					
Topic Development					
Topic Termination					
Language Use					
Delivery					
Overall Evaluation					

Unit 9

Cybersecurity

Part 1

Science ABC

Task 1: Dictation

Directions: Listen to a recording entitled *How one company refused to let cyberattackers win* and complete the excerpt with one word in each space.

> **New Words & Phrases**
> 1. drill: *n.* a way of learning something by means of repeated exercises 训练
> 2. infrastructure: *n.* the basic systems and services that are necessary for a country or an organization to run smoothly, for example buildings, transport and water and power supplies 基础设施
> 3. brittle: *adj.* hard but easily broken 脆弱的
> 4. extort: *v.* to make somebody give you something by threatening them 敲诈
> 5. encrypt: *v.* to put information into a special code, especially in order to prevent people from looking at it without authority 加密

In March 2019, the day after Hilde Merete Aasheim was appointed CEO of a company that produces enough energy in Norway for 1. _____ homes per day, she received a call at 4 a.m. "We are under a severe 2. _____. You have to come to work." Critical 3. _____ systems around the globe have become a favorite target of 4. _____ organizations.

Last May's attack on Colonial Pipeline, a major oil provider on the East Coast of the U.S., showed not only how 5. _____ corporate cybersecurity standards can be but also that integral businesses can potentially be extorted into paying ransoms. But "paying a ransom offers no 6. _____ that a victim organization will regain access to their data or have their 7. _____ data returned," says Eric Goldstein, "Ransomware is a criminal economy—and as long as victims are paying ransom, we can expect these criminal groups to be further incentivized to conduct ongoing attacks."

The attack against Hydro infected its global network of nearly 3,000 computers and 8. _____ key areas of the company's IT network. It stalled production in most of its manufacturing facilities. But paying the hackers to regain access could have left the company with a 9. _____ system—and receptive to another attack. "There was never the 10. _____ to pay any ransom," says Aasheim. So Hydro shut down its network and took up the task of removing the virus from the equation altogether.

Task 2: True or False

Directions: Listen to a recording entitled *Health data and privacy* and decide if the following statements are true or false. Write down T for True and F for False.

> **New Words & Phrases**
> 1. pandemic: *n.* a disease that spreads over a whole country or the whole world 流行病
> 2. repository: *n.* a place where something is stored in large quantities 储藏室
> 3. asthma: *n.* a medical condition of the chest that makes breathing difficult 哮喘
> 4. ingenuity: *n.* the ability to invent things or solve problems in clever new ways 足智多谋
> 5. trove: *n.* a place, book, etc. containing many useful or beautiful things 宝库

1. An article appeared on medRxiv claimed that for England at least, women who suffered from SARS-CoV-2 are more likely to die than men who suffered from the same virus. _____

2. Current smokers are less likely to die from the illness than non-smokers do. _____

3. In the past, British people were concerned with making plans related with primary care data. _____

4. It took OpenSAFELY over a year to go from idea to publication. _____

5. The research was carried out by studying the medical records of about 17m people on the books of GPs in England and over 5,000 COVID-19-attributable deaths. _____

Task 3: Multiple Choices

Directions: Watch a video entitled *Unprecedented Hack on Twitter* and choose the best answer.

> **New Words & Phrases**
> 1. compromise: *v.* to bring someone or something/yourself into danger or under suspicion 破坏，使陷入危险，使受到怀疑
> 2. Twitter: *n.* now called "X" 推特（现称为 X 平台）

1. Which of the following celebrity is not involved in this cyber scam?
A. Bill Gates.
B. Elon Musk.
C. The host.

2. What did the victims do?
A. They sent tens of thousands of dollars to a single account.
B. They got twice the money they sent in return.
C. They posted what happened to them online.

3. What did Twitter do in response?
A. They reported to President Joe Biden.
B. They prevented verified accounts from tweeting.
C. They closed off the website.

Part 2

Science News

Task 4: Moves and Details

Directions: Listen to a short piece of science news entitled *How to Keep COVID-19 Conspiracies Contained* and fill up blanks for each move.

New Words & Phrases
1. conspiracy: *n.* a secret plan by a group of people to do something harmful or illegal 阴谋
2. gravitate towards: to move towards somebody/something that you are attracted to 被吸引
3. dislodge: *v.* to force or knock something out of its position 驱逐
4. inoculate: *v.* to protect a person or an animal from catching a particular disease by injecting them with a mild form of the disease 接种

Moves	Details
Finding	Along with COVID-19, something else is spreading across America: 1. c_____ theories.
Reason	People are 2.p_____ detectors.
Method	They recently released a guide called *How to 3.S_____ COVID-19 Conspiracy Theories*. The key is to identify the 4.h_____ of conspiratorial thinking.
Result	A better approach is to inoculate people against 5.m_____ by explaining what to look for in advance.

Task 5: News Retelling

Directions: Work with your partners and retell the news based on the moves in the table.

Part 3

Lecture

New Words & Phrases

1. adversary: *n.* a person that somebody is opposed to and competing with in an argument or a battle 对手，敌手
2. omnipresent: *adj.* present everywhere 无处不在的

Task 6: Listening Comprehension

Directions: Watch part of a lecture entitled *Introduction: Threat Models* and answer the following three types of questions.

Basic Comprehension Questions

1. What is this lecture mainly about?

_____

Pragmatic Understanding Questions

2. What is the purpose of mentioning that "we need to think about what the bad guy is going to do?"

_____

3. What does the professor imply when he says "better to err on the side of caution and being conservative"?

_____

Connecting Information Questions

4. How does the professor clarify "integrity"?

_____

5. Why does the professor make a comparison between TAs who can access the grades and non-TAs who try to access the grades illegally?

_____

Task 7: Lecture Structure

Directions: Watch the video again and fill in the lecture notes.

Introduction:

What is security?
  • Achieve some goal in the presence of an 1. a _____.
  • Build a system 2. r_____ to a whole range of bad guys.

High-level plan for thinking about security:
- Policy: the goal you want to achieve
  - ✓ e.g., only I or TAs are able to read 3. g____ files for 6.858.
  - ✓ typical goals: 4. c_____, 5. i_____, 6. a_____.
- Threat model: assumptions about the bad guy
  - ✓ e.g., bad guy doesn't know your 7. p_____ or have physical 8. a_____ to your phone
  - ✓ better to 9. e_____ on the side of being 10. c_____ in picking your system
- Mechanism: make sure the policy is followed as long as bad guys follow the model
- Ending result: no way for adversary within threat model to violate policy

Speech

Task 8: Speech Organization

Directions: Watch a TED talk entitled *Where is cybercrime really coming from* and answer the following questions.

New Words & Phrases
1. espionage: *n.* the activity of secretly getting important political or military information about another country or of finding out another company's secrets by using spies 间谍活动
2. regimented: *adj.* involving strict discipline and/or organization 编成团的，非常严格的
3. peddle: *v.* to try to sell goods by going from house to house or from place to place 兜售

> **Topic Introduction-Problem**

1. How does the presenter introduce his topic?

_____

> **Topic Development**

Topic Development-Cause

2. What is widely-held misperception about the cause of this problem?

_____

3. Where are most of online crimes from?

_____

4. What is the purpose of telling the Dyre Wolf story?

_____

5. What problem may occur when you are issuing a wire transfer?

_____

6. What is the dark web?

_____

Topic Development-Solution

7. What is the best way to solve the problem?

_____

8. What are the benefits of this solution?

_____

9. What actions did the speaker take?

_____

> **Topic Termination**

10. How does the speaker end his speech?

Task 9: Speech Outline

Directions: Please design a mind map in the box with your group and show the clear structure of this speech. You may refer to the questions in Task 8.

Task 10: Language Use

Directions: Watch the following clips of this video again and discuss the following questions with your partners.

Clip 1(00:00-00:45)
1. How does the speaker highlight the significance of the problem?

Clip 2(01:39-02:32)
2. How does the speaker explain "445 billion dollars" to the audience?

Clip 3(02:32-04: 56)
3. While explaining how criminals work, the speaker engages "you" in the story. What is the possible effect in speech making?

Clip 4 (06:27-07:12)
4. Why does the speaker mention Yelp and Tripadvisor?

Clip 5(09:10-09:58)
5. Why does the speaker mention SARS, Ebola and bird flu?

Task 11: Discussion

Directions: Analyze the delivery skills of this speech and discuss with your partners. You may refer to the following points.

1. The speaker's body

(1) Personal appearance

(2) Eye contact

(3) Body movement

2. The speaker's voice

(1) Volume

(2) Rate

(3) Pauses

(4) Vocal variety

3. Visual aids

(1) Objects and models

(2) PowerPoint

Part 5

Oral Practice

Task 12: Group Presentation

Directions: Make a presentation on the topic of cybersecurity with your group. The rest of students fill out the following evaluation form.

Presentation Evaluation Form

Items	5-Excellent	4-Good	3-Average	2-Fair	1-Poor
Topic Introduction					
Topic Development					
Topic Termination					
Language Use					
Delivery					
Overall Evaluation					

Unit 10

Metaverse

Part 1

Science ABC

Task 1: Dictation

Directions: Listen to a recording entitled *Zuckerberg announced the rebrand of Facebook as Meta* and complete the excerpt with one word in each space.

> **New Words & Phrases**
> 1. dystopian: *adj.* of or pertaining to or resembling a dystopia 反乌托邦的
> 2. coin: *v.* to invent a new word or phrase that other people then begin to use 创造（新词语）
> 3. address: *v.* to make a formal speech to a group of people 演说，演讲
> 4. ticker: *n.* a machine that prints out data on a strip of paper, especially stock market information（股票行情等的）自动收报机，股票代码
> 5. namesake: *n.* a person or thing that has the same name as another 同名者（物），同姓者

As he faces scrutiny from lawmakers and regulators at home and abroad, Facebook CEO Mark Zuckerberg on Thursday announced a rebrand of the company he 1. _____ in 2004: "Our company is now Meta." The name change comes as the world's largest social media company 2. _____ criticism over its market power, algorithm and abuse on its platforms. Speaking at the company's live-streamed virtual and augmented reality conference, Zuckerberg said it reflects the company's ambitions to build the metaverse, which it bets will be the 3. _____ to the mobile Internet.

A term coined in a dystopian novel three decades ago and now 4. _____in Silicon Valley, metaverse refers broadly to the idea of a shared virtual environment. The company, which has invested 5. _____ in augmented and virtual reality, said the change would bring together its different apps and technologies under one new brand, and would not change its corporate 6. _____. With about 2.9 billion monthly users, the company has faced increased scrutiny. Especially after Facebook employee Frances Haugen leaked documents, she said, showed the company chose profit 7. _____ user safety. Zuckerberg earlier this week said the documents were being used to paint a "false picture."

On Thursday, as Zuckerberg addressed the conference, the company 8. _____ a new sign at its headquarters in Menlo Park, California, replacing its thumbs-up "Like" logo with a blue 9. _____ icon. Its stock ticker will also change to MVRS on December 1st. But the company's 10. _____ social media service will continue to be called Facebook.

Task 2: True or False

Directions: Listen to a recording entitled *Microsoft's Acquisition of Activision Blizzard* and decide if the following statements are true or false. Write down T for True and F for False.

> **New Words & Phrases**
>
> 1. share: *n.* any of the units of equal value into which a company is divided and sold to raise money 股份
>
> 2. at a premium: at a higher than normal price 超出平常价，溢价
>
> 3. scoop up: take out or up with or as if with a scoop（敏捷地）抱起来，收购
>
> 4. edge: *n.* a quality or factor which gives superiority over close rivals or competitors 优势
>
> 5. slump: *v.* undergo a sudden severe or prolonged fall in price, value, or amount（价格、价值或数量的）猛然严重下跌，长期下跌
>
> 6. allegation: *n.* a claim or assertion that someone has done something illegal or wrong, typically one made without proof（尤指无证据的）宣称，指控，假说
>
> 7. discipline: *v.* to punish sb. for sth. they have done 惩罚，处罚

1. Microsoft announced it was acquiring Activision Blizzard for $58.7 billion in cash._____

2. Microsoft's offer of $95 per share is at a premium of 45% to Activision's Friday close. _____

3. "Minecraft" made by Mojang Studios and Zenimax give Microsoft's Xbox platform an edge over Sony's Playstation. _____

4. According to Microsoft CEO Satya Nadella, gaming will play a key role in the development of metaverse platforms._____

5. Activision on Monday said the allegations of sexual harassment and other misconduct at the company have all been tackled well._____

Task 3: Multiple Choices

Directions: Watch a video entitled *What is the Metaverse?* and choose the best answer.

> **New Words & Phrases**
>
> 1. buzzword: *n.* a word or phrase, especially one connected with a particular subject, that has become fashionable and popular and is used a lot in newspapers, etc.（报刊等的）时髦术语
>
> 2. immersive: *adj.* used to describe a computer system or image that seems to surround the user（计算机系统或图像）沉浸式虚拟现实的
>
> 3. brainstorm: *v.* (of a group of people) to all think about something at the same time, often in order to solve a problem or to create good ideas 头脑风暴，集思广益
>
> 4. fully-fledged: *adj.* completely developed; with all the qualifications necessary for sth.成熟的，完全合格的

1. Which of the following is not the meaning of the term "metaverse"?

A. Online spaces allowing people to interact in a more immersive way than a traditional website.

B. A virtual next life where one person can be anyone and do anything without any bounds.

C. Virtual environments where you have an avatar and could interact with other people's avatars.

2. Which products has Facebook invested heavily in developing, to bring its metaverse plan to life?

A. VR and AR headsets and glasses.

B. High-speed wireless communication routers.

C. Smart IoT sensors.

3. Which of the following statements is TRUE?

A. Microsoft hasn't thought about converging the digital and physical worlds.

B. The blockchain technology supporting Decentraland is different from that behind bitcoin.

C. Fully-fledged metaverses almost indistinguishable from real physical life are still far away.

Part 2

Science News

Task 4: Moves and Details

Directions: Listen to a short piece of science news entitled *VR might help those who suffer from dementia* and fill up blanks for each move.

New Words & Phrases
1. pedal: *n.* a flat bar on a machine such as a bicycle, car, etc. that you push down with your foot in order to make parts of the machine move or work（自行车等）的踏板
2. dementia: *n.* a serious mental disorder caused by brain disease or injury, that affects the ability to think, remember and behave normally 痴呆，精神错乱
3. cardio: *n.* physical exercise that increases the rate at which your heart breaks 有氧运动

Moves	Details
Motivation	Garcia says he remembers how his parents and grandparents all suffered from 1.d_____ , when they could not take care of themselves, like paying the bills, driving, cooking for themselves, dressing themselves.
Purpose	Researchers want to see if just a small amount of VR can help 2._____ memory loss as people age.
Method	He starts by putting on virtual reality (VR) 3.e_____ on his head. He then gets on a 4.s_____ designed exercise bicycle and starts pushing its pedals.
Result	VR provides a first-person, three-dimensional 5.e_____ that is important to memory training.

Task 5: News Retelling

Directions: Work with your partners and retell the news based on the moves in the table.

Lecture

New Words & Phrases

1. composite: *adj.* made of different parts or materials 合成的，复合的

2. agency: *n.* a thing or person that acts to produce a particular result 起作用的事物（或人）

3. immersion: *n.* the state of being completely involved in sth. 沉浸，专心，陷入

4. haptic: *adj.* relating to or involving the sense of touch 触觉的，与触觉有关的

5. olfactory: *adj.* connected with the sense of smell 嗅觉的

6. align: *v.* to arrange sth. in the correct position, or to be in the correct position, in relation to sth. else, especially in a straight line 排整齐，校准

7. continuum: *n.* a set of things on a scale, which have a particular characteristics to different degrees 连续统一体

Task 6: Listening Comprehension

Directions: Watch part of a lecture entitled *What is XR?* and answer the following three types of questions.

Basic Comprehension Questions

1. What is the main topic of this lecture?

_____

Pragmatic Understanding Questions

2. What does the lecturer imply when he says this "the R in VR is actually not the real world"?

_____

3. What is the purpose of saying "Mixed Reality is a term that often causes confusion"?

_____

Connecting Information Questions

4. How does the lecturer explain the first characteristics of AR?

_____

5. Why does the lecturer show the audience a number of examples of displays as they map to the spectrum?

_____

Task 7: Lecture Structure

Directions: Watch the video again and fill in the lecture notes.

Introduction:

Three main characteristics of virtual reality (VR):

- VR emphasizes autonomy and agency.
  - ✓ The user at all times stays in 1. c_____.
  - ✓ Through head tracking and using the 2. b_____ as input.
- VR provides natural interaction.
- VR give us a sense of 3. p_____ by stimulating multiple of our senses.

Three main characteristics of augmented reality (AR):

- AR combines real and virtual objects to produce a 4. c_____ view.
- AR is interactive in real time. It supports both explicit and 5. i_____ interaction.
- AR is 6. r_____ in 3D to align the real and virtual objects.

Definition of mixed reality (XR) by Milgram in terms of the reality-virtuality continuum:

- A spectrum from the real environment without any augmentation to the virtual environment, which is completely 7. s_____ computer-generated virtual content.
- A 8. b_____ of the physical and the virtual world with varying degrees of augmentation.

XR in terms of displays:

- Closer towards the real environment: 9. t_____ interactive displays or spatially projective displays.
- Between AR to AV: tablets and smartphones.
- Closer towards the virtual environment: CAVEs-room size, wall size, displays around the user, or a head 10. m_____ display.

Part 4

Speech

Task 8: Speech Organization

Directions: Watch a TED talk entitled *How NFTs are building the Internet of the future* and answer the following questions.

New Words & Phrases

1. fad: *n.* something that people are interested in for only a short period of time 一时的狂热

2. burgeoning: *adj.* rapidly growing or developing 迅速发展的，快速生长的

3. prescient: *adj.* knowing or appearing to know about things before they happen 预知的

4. mediate: *v.* to influence sth. and/or make it possible for it to happen 影响……的发生

5. encumbrance: *n.* a person or thing that prevents sb. from moving easily or from doing what they want 妨碍者，累赘，障碍物

6. meme: *n.* an image, video, etc. that is passed electronically from one Internet user to another 模因，网络话题

➤ **Topic Introduction-Announce Topic**

1. How does the speaker introduce his topic?

_____

➤ **Topic Development**

Topic Development-Introduce History

2. What did many people think of Internet back in 1992?

_____

3. What is the pitfall inherent in Internet as seen by John Perry Barlow?

_____

4. Have people found solution to issues like property and ownership, as the Internet increasingly became their default context after 1992?

_____

5. Who control most of the value on today's Internet?

_____

Topic Development-Definition & Explanation

6. What is an NFT?

_____

7. What is the different between ownership in the physical world and that offered by NFTs?

_____

112

Topic Development-Solution

8. Why could the creators continue to receive compensation every single time the NFT is resold?

_____

9. What does the speaker mean by saying that NFTs are portable?

_____

➤ **Topic Termination**

10. How does the speaker end his speech?

_____

Task 9: Speech Outline

Directions: Please design a mind map in the box with your group and show the clear structure of this speech. You may refer to the questions in Task 8.

_____

Task 10: Language Use

Directions: Watch the following clips of this video again and discuss the following questions with your partners.

Clip 1(01:56-03:11)

1. How does the speaker explain "why none of the early approaches failed to protect property and ownership"?

_____

Clip 2(04:02-04:51)

2. How does the speaker explain to audience "What is an NFT"?

_____

Clip 3(05:16-06:14)

3. What's the purpose of the speaker using an example to clarify the feature of NFT: *the more an NFT is seen, appreciated and understood, the more possibility it has to increase in value*?

_____

Clip 4 (07:12-07:56)

4. Why does the speaker mention Yatreda, the Ethiopian artist collective?

_____

Clip 5(09:07-09:38)

5. What sentence pattern does the writer use in concluding his speech and why?

_____

Task 11: Discussion

Directions: Analyze the delivery skills of this speech and discuss with your partners. You may refer to the following points.

1. The speaker's body

(1) Personal appearance

(2) Eye contact

(3) Body movement

2. The speaker's voice

(1) Volume

(2) Rate

(3) Pauses

(4) Vocal variety

3. Visual aids

(1) Objects and models

(2) PowerPoint

Part 5

Oral Practice

Task 12: Group Presentation

Directions: Make a presentation on the topic of metaverse with your group. The rest of students fill out the following evaluation form.

Presentation Evaluation Form

Items	5-Excellent	4-Good	3-Average	2-Fair	1-Poor
Topic Introduction					
Topic Development					
Topic Termination					
Language Use					
Delivery					
Overall Evaluation					

Unit **11**

Cloud Computing

Science ABC

Task 1: Dictation

Directions: Listen to a recording entitled *Innovative Tech in Class* and complete the excerpt with one word in each space.

New Words & Phrases
1. collaborate: *v.* to work together with a person or group in order to achieve something, especially in science or art 合作，协作
2. sitcom: *n.* (situation comedy) a funny television programme in which the same characters appear in different situations each week 情景喜剧
3. air: *v.* to broadcast a programme on television or radio 播出
4. chatbot: *n.* a computer program designed to send messages back to a human user, as if it is having a conversation 聊天机器人
5. flip: *v.* to move something with a sudden quick movement so that it is in a different position 翻转

... Ding Talk, QQ, Zoom and others have been the 1._____ platforms for online courses. But while we're slowly returning to everyday life, our fast adoption of online resources for teaching has proven that the reality of the cloud classroom might not be far away. The idea of the cloud classroom, or cloud learning, is that all the required resources for a class are 2._____ and can be 3._____ via the cloud from anywhere in the world. It will allow learners to communicate and collaborate on projects in real-time and give educators the chance to integrate more 4._____ class activities.

In an episode of the US animated sitcom The Simpsons, ... While the episode first 5._____ in 1993, this glimpse into the future still holds with the modern-day aspirations of the cloud classroom. With the coming of 5G, cloud computing will 6._____ a range of exciting technologies in the education field. Among the best-known technologies is VR.... According to Forbes, 7._____ reality including virtual, increased, and mixed reality brings immersive learning experiences to students no matter where they are.

Another innovation is the 8._____ of chatbots.... Chatbots can be used as a tool to answer questions and deliver 9._____ lectures according to the learner's needs. According to AI product developer Bernhard Schindlholzer, VR and AI use can allow for "flipped learning", ... "With cloud computing students are challenged to apply their knowledge to real-world problems ... the traditional mode of 10._____ knowledge and then examining will be a thing of the past," he stated ....

Task 2: True or False

Directions: Listen to a recording entitled *Cloud Computing Role* and decide if the following statements are true or false. Write down T for True and F for False.

New Words & Phrases
1. primary: *adj.* most important 首要的
2. ecosystem: *n.* all the animals and plants in a particular area, and the way in which they are related to each other and to their environment 生态系统
3. designate: *v.* to choose someone or something for a particular job or purpose 任命

1. There are three primary roles for cloud computing. _____

2. The primary roles in the world of cloud computing include cloud service provider and the cloud customer. _____

3. Cloud service providers use cloud services as the infrastructure, platforms, and/or applications that help them run their own business. _____

4. A cloud customer may never interact with employees at a cloud provider. _____

5. A cloud service partner might assist a company only in implementing a cloud application. _____

Task 3: Multiple Choices

Directions: Watch a video entitled *What is cloud computing* and choose the best answer.

New Words & Phrases
1. bandwidth: *n.* the amount of information that can be carried through a telephone wire, computer connection etc. at one time (计算机) 带宽
2. configure: *v.* to arrange something, especially computer equipment, so that it works with other equipment (计算机) 配置
3. customize: *v.* to change something to make it more suitable for you, or to make it look special or different from things of a similar type 定制
4. tenancy: *n.* an act of being a tenant or occupant 租赁
5. elastic: *adj.* able to adjust readily to different conditions 有弹性的，灵活的
6. subscription: *n.* an amount of money you pay, usually once a year, to receive copies of a newspaper or magazine, or receive a service, or the act of paying money for this 订阅

1. Which of the following is NOT the things needed by business apps to run businesses?

A. A data center.

B. Staff and a team of experts.

C. Right chances.

2. Why is cloud computing a better way to run your business?

A. They run on a shared data center.

B. They are only used for business apps.

C. They need to be upgraded once in a while.

3. Why do businesses run all kinds of apps in the cloud these days?

A. They share similarities with traditional apps.

B. They can be up and running quickly and cost less.

C. Cloud will eat up your IT resources.

Part 2

Science News

Task 4: Moves and Details

Directions: Listen to a short piece of science news entitled *Online Medical Care* and fill up blanks for each move.

New Words & Phrases
1. telemedicine: *n.* the use of telecommunication and information technologies in order to provide clinical health care at a distance 远程医疗
2. diagnose: *v.* determine or distinguish the nature of a problem or an illness through a diagnostic analysis 诊断
3. forum: *n.* a public meeting or assembly for open discussion 论坛
4. advent: *n.* arrival that has been awaited (especially of something momentous) 到来，问世
5. relent: *v.* to become less severe 减轻，好转

Moves	Details
Problem	With the spread of COVID-19, there is more need for doctors than what is available around the world. According to statistics from the WHO in 2017, 1. China has _____ medical doctors per 10,000 people, the US has _____, and the UK has _____.
Solution	The rise of 2. _____ allows doctors to make better use of their time and provides better healthcare access.
Advantage	With cloud computing, 3. _____ can be easily shared and updated by all healthcare providers, and a patient's key signs can be 4. _____ from their homes.
Effect	Telemedicine will allow for more 5._____ of patients long after COVID-19 pandemic has relented.

Task 5: News Retelling

Directions: Work with your partners and retell the news based on the moves in the table.

120

Lecture

> **New Words & Phrases**
> 1. trendy: *adj.* in accord with the latest fad 时髦的
> 2. outsource: *v.* obtain goods or services from an outside supplier 外包
> 3. RAM: *n.* (random access memory) the part of a computer that acts as a temporary store for information so that it can be used immediately 内存，随机存储器
> 4. nebulous: *adj. formal* unclear and has no definite edges 模糊的，不清楚的
> 5. pictorially: *adv.* in a pictorial manner 绘画般地
> 6. server: *n.* the main computer on a network, which controls all the others 服务器
> 7. finite: *adj.* having an end or a limit 有限的
> 8. headroom: *n.* the amount of available resources (such as processing power, memory, storage, or network bandwidth) beyond what is currently being utilized,essentially the spare capacity or overhead that a server has before it reaches its maximum performance or capacity limits 性能余量，资源余量，空间余量

Task 6: Listening Comprehension

Directions: Watch part of a lecture entitled *Cloud Computing* and answer the following three types of questions.

Basic Comprehension Questions

1. What is this lecture mainly about?

Pragmatic Understanding Questions

2. What is the purpose of giving out simple scenarios at the beginning of the speech?

---

3. What does the professor imply when he mentions that it is bad if the server cannot hold the load?

Connecting Information Questions

4. What are limits to the load of a server?

---

5. According to the professor, what would happen if we simply address similar names to different servers?

Task 7: Lecture Structure

Directions: Watch the video again and fill in the lecture notes.

Introduction:

What is cloud computing?

- Renting 1. s_____ and renting time on someone else's computers.
- Putting more and more 2. h_____ off site, so that companies no longer need to host their own physical hardware or roles in their own local companies.

We need cloud computing to solve:

- Problem 1: when load of one server hits the upper limit:
  - ✓ When you can't handle all of the 3. l_____, costumers aren't able to 4. v_____ your website.
  - ✓ The intuitive solution is to add another 5. s_____ with the same 6. s_____.
- Problem 2: how do we direct traffic to different servers:
  - ✓ When you give similar names to the URLs, you're trying to build some 7. b_____ around your URL.
  - ✓ You get fancier, bigger servers that can handle more users and you 8. g_____ with some of them. If customers bookmarked one of those older names, they might hit a 9. d_____.

Closing: It would be nice to do this a little more 10. t_____.

Speech

Task 8: Speech Organization

Directions: Watch a TED talk entitled *Where's My Data? Implications of Cloud Computing for You!* and answer the following questions.

New Words & Phrases

1. headline: *n.* the title of a newspaper report, which is printed in large letters above the report（报纸的）大标题

2. entrenched: *adj.* strongly established and not likely to change, often used to show disapproval 根深蒂固的

3. fluffy: *adj.* not serious or important 空洞的，不严肃的

4. momentum: *n.* the ability to keep increasing, developing, or being more successful 动力，势头

5. agility: *n.* the gracefulness of a person or animal that is quick and nimble 敏捷性

➢ **Topic Introduction-Problem**

1. How does the speaker introduce his topic?

_____

2. What is the business of the speaker?

_____

3. What are the main contents for today's speech?

_____

➢ **Topic Development**
Topic Development-Argument

4. What changes does cloud computing bring about?

_____

5. What is the key reason for organizations to move into cloud computing?

_____

Topic Development-Exemplification

6. What are the two examples that the speaker provides to explain the key reason for organizations to move into cloud computing?

_____

7. Why do companies need to adopt cloud computing?

_____

8. What is the speaker's second thesis?

_____

9. Where would almost all data be stored in a decade, according to the speaker?

_____

> **Topic Termination**
10. What is the key point in the summary?

_____

Task 9: Speech Outline

Directions: Please design a mind map in the box with your group and show the clear structure of this speech. You may refer to the questions in Task 8.

```



```

Task 10: Language Use

Directions: Watch the following clips of this video again and discuss the following questions with your partners.

Clip 1(00:05-01:37)
1. Why does the speaker mention that the Pentagon or Dutch bank is investing millions or even billions of US dollars into cloud computing?

_____

Clip 2(03:18-03:48)
2. According to your understanding, what does "hyperscalers" mean in this part?

_____

Clip 3(05:08-06:33)
3. Why does the speaker mention his own business here?

_____

Clip 4 (08:55-09:39)
4. How does the speaker bring out his first thesis?

_____

124

Clip 5(12:21-13:37)

5. What is the speaker's attitude towards data security?

_____

Task 11: Discussion

Directions: Analyze the delivery skills of this speech and discuss with your partners. You may refer to the following points.

1. The speaker's body

(1) Personal appearance

(2) Eye contact

(3) Body movement

2. The speaker's voice

(1) Volume

(2) Rate

(3) Pauses

(4) Vocal variety

3. Visual aids

(1) Objects and models

(2) PowerPoint

Oral Practice

Task 12: Group Presentation

Directions: Make a presentation on the topic of cloud computing with your group. The rest of students fill out the following evaluation form.

Presentation Evaluation Form

Items	5-Excellent	4-Good	3-Average	2-Fair	1-Poor
Topic Introduction					
Topic Development					
Topic Termination					
Language Use					
Delivery					
Overall Evaluation					

Unit 12

Unmanned Aerial Vehicle

Science ABC

Task 1: Dictation

Directions: Listen to a recording entitled *The Rise of Drones (1)* and complete the excerpt with one word in each blank.

New Words & Phrases
drone: *n.* an aircraft without a pilot, controlled from the ground, used for taking photographs, dropping bombs, delivering goods, etc. 无人驾驶飞机

[Neil] Hello. And today we're discussing those 1. _____ aircraft that we seem to be hearing and reading a lot about at the 2. _____.

[Rob] You mean drones. And yes, they are in the news quite often for good and bad reasons. They've been used for many things from 3. _____ drugs, detecting water 4. _____ and surveillance.

[Neil] And surveillance, that means "the act of 5. _____ watching someone or something", perhaps a 6. _____. But also it means 7. _____, maybe on me and you, Rob. So should we be welcoming the 8. _____ of the use of drones?

[Rob] Well, before our discussion about that "takes off", we need to set today's question for you to answer, Neil.

[Neil] What are you droning on about, Rob? And by that I don't mean "flying a drone", I mean "talking too much in a very 9. _____ way"!

[Rob] Thanks Neil. Now just answer this, will you? Drones are sometimes also 10. _____ to as UAVs. So, what does UAV stand for? Is it a) unidentified aerial vehicle, b) unmanned aerial vehicle, or c) unaided aircraft vehicle?

[Neil] Well, I'm going to go for b) unmanned aerial vehicle.

Task 2: True or False

Directions: Listen to a recording entitled *The Rise of Drones (2)* and decide if the following statements are true or false. Write down T for True and F for False.

New Words & Phrases
1. hazard: *n.* a thing that can be dangerous or cause damage 危险，隐患
2. near miss: *n.* a narrowly avoided collision 侥幸避开的相撞
3. footage: *n.* part of a film showing a particular event （描述某一事件的）片段镜头
4. on the flip side: looking at a different or opposite aspect 反过来说，另一方面

1. In 2016 in the UK there were 70 accidents involving drones. _____

2. Camera attached to drones are good at aerial filming. _____

3. Drones were used to inspect the inside of the damaged Fukushima Nuclear Power Station. _____

4. UNICEF and the Malawian government test drones for carrying food supplies. _____

5. A Japanese firm plans to use a drone to force employees to work extra hours. _____

Task 3: Multiple Choices

Directions: Watch a video entitled *US Military Drones* and choose the best answer.

New Words & Phrases
1. Predator:（美军）"捕食者"无人机
2. MQ-9 Reaper:（美军）"死神"无人机
3. Hellfire missile:（美军）"地狱火"反坦克导弹
4. The Intercept: an award-winning news organization 美国调查新闻网站"拦截者"
5. retrieval: *n.* the process of getting something back, especially from a place where it should not be 取回，收回
6. antenna: *n.* a piece of equipment made of wire or long straight pieces of metal for receiving or sending radio and television signals 天线

1. The most powerful US military drone that can carry out attacks is _____.

A. the Predator

B. the Reaper

C. the Global Hawk

2. A crew has likely been monitoring a target for _____ by the time a drone strike is ordered.

A. hours

B. days

C. weeks

3. Which of the following statements is TRUE?

A. In some cases the orders of drone strikes should be approved by the US President.

B. Drones are piloted remotely and require no ground crew for launch.

C. Satellite communication systems on drones allow ground crew to control take-off and landing.

Science News

Task 4: Moves and Details

Directions: Listen to a short piece of science news entitled *Drones Could Help Biologists Tally Birds* and fill in blanks for each move.

New Words & Phrases

1. ecologist: *n.* a scientist who studies ecology 生态学家

2. binoculars: *n.* an optical instrument designed for simultaneous use by both eyes 双筒望远镜

3. tally: *v.* to calculate the total number, cost, etc. of sth. 合计，统计

4. roost: *n.* a place where birds sleep （鸟类的）栖息处

5. avian: *adj.* of or connected with birds 鸟（类）的

6. pod: *n.* a small group of animals, especially seals, whales, or birds 一小群动物

7. poach: *v.* to illegally hunt birds, animals or fish on sb. else's property or without permission （在他人地界）偷猎，偷捕

8. replica: *n.* a very good or exact copy of sth. 复制品，仿制品

9. colony: *n.* a group of plants or animals that live together or grow in the same place （同地生长的植物或动物）群，群体

10. decoy: *n.* an animal or a bird, or a model of one, that attracts other animals or birds, especially so that they can be shot by people who are hunting them （诱捕鸟兽的）动物，假兽，假鸟

11. optimum: *adj.* the best possible; producing the best possible results 最佳的

12. gaggle: *n.* a group of noisy people 一群（吵闹的人）

13. a feather in one's cap: an action that one can be proud of 可引以自豪的行为

Moves	Details
Finding	1. D_____ can do better in getting an accurate avian head count than ecologists.
Research Objective	Whether remote surveys by drones are as 2. a_____ as old-fashioned, feet-on-the-ground, expert evaluations.
Method	Using decoy-sized 3. r_____ ducks, the researchers let some experienced ground counters and a drone count those decoy birds at the same time.
Result	Drone-derived counts made by humans counting the images were more accurate than the traditional ground-based counts. There was no 4. s_____ difference between counts by a computer program and those by our volunteers using exactly the same imagery. Counting by drones not only saves time and effort, but yields better 5. d_____.

Task 5: News Retelling

Directions: Work with your partners and retell the news based on the moves in the table.

Lecture

New Words & Phrases

1. quadcopter: *n.* a type of helicopter with four rotors 四旋翼直升机（quad- 四旋翼的，hexa- 六旋翼的，octa- 八旋翼的）

2. hover: *v.* to stay in the air in one place 盘旋

3. rotorcraft: *n.* an aircraft (such as a helicopter) whose lift is derived principally from rotating airfoils 旋翼飞行器

4. autogyro: *n.* a self-propelled aircraft supported in flight mainly by unpowered rotating horizontal blades 旋翼机

5. actuator: *n.* a component of a machine that is responsible for moving and controlling a mechanism or system, for example by opening a valve 致动器，执行机构

6. ultrasound: *n.* sound that is higher than humans can hear 超声，超音波

7. frame: *n.* one of the single photographs that a film or video is made of 帧

8. inertial: *adj.* connected with or caused by inertia 惯性的

9. translational: *adj.* relating to movement along a line 平移的

10. pitch: *v.* to move up and down in the air 颠簸，俯仰

11. yaw: *v.* to turn to one side, away from a straight course, in an unsteady way 偏航

12. ingenious: *adj.* skillful (or showing skill) in adapting means to ends 精妙的

13. fluid dynamics: 流体动力学

14. torque: *n.* a twisting force that causes machinery, etc. to rotate （使机器等旋转的）转矩

15. flesh out: add details, as to an account or idea 使其更完整、更具体

Task 6: Listening Comprehension

Directions: Watch part of a lecture entitled *Designing a Control System for a Quadcopter* and answer the following three types of questions.

Basic Comprehension Questions

1. What is this lecture mainly about?

_____

2. What is special about the quadcopter's spin direction?

_____

3. Why does the lecturer say the quadcopter is an under-actuated system?

_____

Pragmatic Understanding Questions

4. What is the purpose of mentioning that "even if you don't plan on writing your own drone controller, it's worth understanding the process"?

_____

Connecting Information Questions

5. Why does the lecturer elaborate on the sensors and actuators of the quadcopter before talking about the control system?

_____

Task 7: Lecture Structure

Directions: Watch the video again and fill in the lecture notes.

Introduction:

What is a quadcopter?

- It's named so because of its four rotating 1. p _____.
- A member of the 2. r_____ family.

Understanding quadcopters:

- Sensors:
    - ✓ Ultrasound sensors used to measure 3. v_____ distances.
    - ✓ A camera able to estimate 4. h_____ motion and speed.
    - ✓ A pressure sensor measuring 5. a_____.
    - ✓ An IMU measuring linear 6. a_____ and angular rate.
- Actuators
    - ✓ Configuration types: X configuration and 7. p_____ configuration.
    - ✓ Spin direction.

Overview of the control problem:

- How to manipulate the four motors precisely so that the drone can 8. r_____ and maneuver in 3D space.
- Sensors used to directly or indirectly estimate the state of mini drone.
- Developing a controller: an 9. a_____ that runs in software.
- Only four actuators for six degrees of freedom: three translational directions and three 10. r_____ directions.

Speech

Task 8: Speech Organization

Directions: Watch a TED talk entitled *Meet the Dazzling Flying Machines of the Future* and answer the following questions.

New Words & Phrases

1. tether: *v.* to tie an animal to a post so that it cannot move very far 拴（牲畜）

2. tensile: *adj.* that can be drawn out or stretched 可拉长的，能伸长的，可延展的

3. ETH Zurich: 苏黎世联邦理工学院

4. spin-off: *n.* an unexpected but useful result of an activity that is designed to produce sth. else （意外但有用的）副产品，派生物

5. tail-sitter: *n.* a type of vertical take-off and landing aircraft that takes off and lands on its tail, then tilts horizontally for forward flight 尾坐式垂直起落飞机

6. have your cake and eat it: (*idiom.*) to have the advantages of something without its disadvantages; to have both things that are available 鱼与熊掌兼得

7. susceptible: *adj.* very likely to be influenced, harmed or affected by sb./sth. 易受影响

8. rudder: *n.* a piece of metal at the back of an aircraft that is used for controlling its direction （飞机的）方向舵

9. monospinner: *n.* a controllable flying vehicle with a single moving part 单螺旋无人机

10. aileron: *n.* a part of the wing of a plane that moves up and down to control the plane's balance （飞机的）副翼

11. omnicopter: *n.* a twin-bladed tilt-rotor aircraft with three blades on each wing 全方向无人机

12. ambivalent: *adj.* having or showing both positive and negative feelings about sb./sth. 矛盾的，模棱两可的

13. quadrocopter: *n.* a drone with four rotors, each with a motor and propeller 四角直升机

14. albeit: *conj.* although 尽管，虽然

15. palette: *n.* a thin board with a hole in it for the thumb to go through, used by an artist for mixing colours on when painting 调色板

16. lampshade: *n.* a decorative cover for a lamp that is used to make the light softer or to direct it 灯罩

17. nascent: *adj.* beginning to exist; not yet fully developed 新生的，萌芽的

18. icing on the cake: (*idiom.*) something extra and not essential that is added to an already good situation or experience and that makes it even better 锦上添花

➤ **Topic Introduction-Theme**

1. How does the speaker introduce his topic?

_____

➤ **Topic Development**

Topic Development-Example 1

2. What are the features of tail-sitters?

_____

3. What is one of the limitations with tail-sitters?

_____

Topic Development-Example 2

4. What is special about the monospinner?

_____

5. What is the shortcoming of the monospinner?

_____

Topic Development-Example 3

6. What are the features of the omnicopter?

_____

Topic Development-Example 4

7. What are the advantages of this quadrocopter-like machine?

_____

Topic Development-Example 5

8. What is the last demonstration about?

_____

➤ **Topic Termination**

9. How does the speaker end his topic?

_____

10. What is the speaker's purpose of showing these five types of drones?

_____

Task 9: Speech Outline

Directions: Please design a mind map in the box with your group and show the clear structure of this speech. You may refer to the questions in Task 8.

Task 10: Language Use

Directions: Watch the following clips of this video again and discuss the following questions with your partners.

Clip 1(00:23-00:53)

1. Why does the speaker show the example of drones building tower of bricks?

_____

Clip 2(02:04-02:32)

2. Why does the speaker say tail-sitter is an aircraft that tries to have its cake and eat it?

_____

Clip 3(03:21-04: 15)

3. How does the speaker introduce the monospinner into his speech?

_____

Clip 4 (05:15-06:38)

4. How does the speaker introduce the omnicopter into his speech?

_____

Clip 5(06:45-07:48)

5. How does the speaker introduce the fourth example into his speech?

_____

Task 11: Discussion

Directions: Analyze the delivery skills of this speech and discuss with your partners. You may refer to the following points.

1. The speaker's body

(1) Personal appearance

(2) Eye contact

(3) Body movement

2. The speaker's voice

(1) Volume

(2) Rate

(3) Pauses

(4) Vocal variety

3. Visual aids

(1) Objects and models

(2) PowerPoint

Part 5

Oral Practice

Task 12: Group Presentation

Directions: Make a presentation on the topic of UAV with your group. The rest of students fill out the following evaluation form.

Presentation Evaluation Form

Items	5-Excellent	4-Good	3-Average	2-Fair	1-Poor
Topic Introduction					
Topic Development					
Topic Termination					
Language Use					
Delivery					
Overall Evaluation					

References

[1] FLOWERDEW J. Academic Listening: Research Perspectives[M]. Cambridge: Cambridge University Press, 1995.

[2] HELGESEN M, BROWN S. Practical English Language Teaching: Listening[M]. New York: The McGraw-Hill Companies, Inc., 2007.

[3] ROST M. Teaching and Researching Listening[M]. Beijing: Foreign Language Teaching and Researching Press, 2005.

[4] ANDERSON K, MACLEAN J, LYNCH T. Study Speaking: A Course in Spoken English for Academic Purposes[M]. Cambridge: Cambridge University Press, 2004.

[5] JORDAN R R. English for Academic Purposes[M]. Cambridge: Cambridge University Press,1997.

[6] HUGHES R, SZCZEPEK R B. Teaching and Researching: Speaking, 3rd Edition[M]. New York: Routledge, 2017.

[7] 陈美华. 学术交流英语[M]. 北京：外语教学与研究出版社，2013.

[8] 范娜. 国际学术交流英语[M]. 北京：清华大学出版社，2019.

[9] 胡庚申. 国际会议交流[M]. 北京：外语教学与研究出版社，2013.

[10] 叶云屏. 理工专业通用学术英语·拓展篇[M]. 北京：北京理工大学出版社，2016.

[11] 张兢田，郭强. 学术英语口语教程[M]. 上海：同济大学出版社，2015.

反侵权盗版声明

　　电子工业出版社依法对本作品享有专有出版权。任何未经权利人书面许可，复制、销售或通过信息网络传播本作品的行为，歪曲、篡改、剽窃本作品的行为，均违反《中华人民共和国著作权法》，其行为人应承担相应的民事责任和行政责任，构成犯罪的，将被依法追究刑事责任。

　　为了维护市场秩序，保护权利人的合法权益，我社将依法查处和打击侵权盗版的单位和个人。欢迎社会各界人士积极举报侵权盗版行为，本社将奖励举报有功人员，并保证举报人的信息不被泄露。

举报电话：（010）88254396；（010）88258888

传　　真：（010）88254397

E-mail：　　dbqq@phei.com.cn

通信地址：北京市海淀区万寿路 173 信箱
　　　　　电子工业出版社总编办公室

邮　　编：100036